Internet Governance

International institutions are evolving quickly as innovative approaches need to be adopted in order to deal with global problems that cannot be successfully addressed by the traditional system of nation-states. The expansion of the Internet has been called the most revolutionary development in the history of human communications. It is ubiquitous and is changing politics, economics, and social relations. Its borderless nature affects the roles of individuals, the magic of the marketplace, and the problems of government regulation. As its development has increased apace, contradictions have arisen between existing regulatory regimes, private interests, government concerns, international norms, and national interests. Unlike most areas where there are global institutions, and the role of governments is predominant, the Internet is a field where the private sector and civil society each have a role as important—or sometimes more important—than governments.

Based on international regime theory, this book analyses how the multi-stakeholder institutions have grown along with the Internet itself. John Mathiason shows how governance of the Internet began as a technical issue but became increasingly political as the management of critical resources began to conflict with other international regimes and the Internet Governance Forum was a compromise solution to a governance issue that did not fit neatly into existing institutional structures. These new institutions will set precedents for other areas where governance is necessary beyond the nation-state.

Internet Governance is an innovative multi-stakeholder approach to dealing with global problems and ideal reading for students, teachers, and researchers of politics of technology, digital politics, and governance.

John Mathiason is Professor of International Relations at the Maxwell School of Citizenship and Public Affairs of Syracuse University. A former official of the United Nations Secretariat, he is the author of *Invisible Governance: International Secretariats in Global Politics* and many articles on global governance.

Routledge Global Institutions

Edited by Thomas G. Weiss
The CUNY Graduate Center, New York, USA
and Rorden Wilkinson
University of Manchester, UK

About the Series

The Global Institutions Series is designed to provide readers with comprehensive, accessible, and informative guides to the history, structure, and activities of key international organizations. Every volume stands on its own as a thorough and insightful treatment of a particular topic, but the series as a whole contributes to a coherent and complementary portrait of the phenomenon of global institutions at the dawn of the millennium.

Books are written by recognized experts, conform to a similar structure, and cover a range of themes and debates common to the series. These areas of shared concern include the general purpose and rationale for organizations, developments over time, membership, structure, decision-making procedures, and key functions. Moreover, current debates are placed in historical perspective alongside informed analysis and critique. Each book also contains an annotated bibliography and guide to electronic information as well as any annexes appropriate to the subject matter at hand.

The volumes currently published or under contract include:

The United Nations and Human Rights (2005)
A guide for a new era
by Julie Mertus (American University)

The UN Secretary General and Secretariat (2005)
by Leon Gordenker (Princeton University)

United Nations Global Conferences (2005)
by Michael G. Schechter (Michigan State University)

The UN General Assembly (2005)
by M.J. Peterson (University of Massachusetts, Amherst)

Internal Displacement (2006)
Conceptualization and its consequences
by Thomas G. Weiss (The CUNY Graduate Center) and David A. Korn

Global Environmental Institutions (2006)
by Elizabeth R. DeSombre (Wellesley College)

The UN Security Council (2006)
Practice and promise
by Edward C. Luck (Columbia University)

The World Intellectual Property Organization (2006)
Resurgence and the development agenda
by Chris May (University of Lancaster)

The North Atlantic Treaty Organization (2007)
The enduring alliance
by Julian Lindley-French (European Union Centre for Security Studies)

The International Monetary Fund (2007)
Politics of conditional lending
by James Raymond Vreeland (Yale University)

The Group of 7/8 (2007)
by Hugo Dobson (University of Sheffield)

The World Economic Forum (2007)
A multi-stakeholder approach to global governance
by Geoffrey Allen Pigman (Bennington College)

The International Committee of the Red Cross (2007)
A neutral humanitarian actor
by David P. Forsythe (University of Nebraska) and Barbara Ann Rieffer-Flanagan (Central Washington University)

The Organization for Security and Co-operation in Europe (2007)
by David J. Galbreath (University of Aberdeen)

United Nations Conference on Trade and Development (UNCTAD) (2007)
by Ian Taylor (University of St. Andrews) and Karen Smith (University of Stellenbosch)

A Crisis of Global Institutions? (2007)
Multilateralism and international security
by Edward Newman (University of Birmingham)

The World Trade Organization (2007)
Law, economics, and politics
by Bernard M. Hoekman (World Bank) and Petros C. Mavroidis (Columbia University)

The African Union (2008)
Challenges of globalization, security, and governance
by Samuel M. Makinda (Murdoch University) and F. Wafula Okumu (Institute for Security Studies)

Commonwealth (2008)
Inter- and non-state contributions to global governance
by Timothy M. Shaw (Royal Roads University and University of the West Indies)

The European Union (2008)
by Clive Archer (Manchester Metropolitan University)

The World Bank (2008)
From reconstruction to development to equity
by Katherine Marshall (Georgetown University)

Contemporary Human Rights Ideas (2008)
by Bertrand G. Ramcharan (Geneva Graduate Institute of International and Development Studies)

The United Nations High Commissioner for Refugees (UNHCR) (2008)
The politics and practice of refugee protection into the twenty-first century
by Gil Loescher (University of Oxford), Alexander Betts (University of Oxford), and James Milner (University of Toronto)

The International Olympic Committee and the Olympic System (2008)
The governance of world sport
by Jean-Loup Chappelet (IDHEAP Swiss Graduate School of Public Administration) and Brenda Kübler-Mabbott

Institutions of the Asia-Pacific (2009)
ASEAN, APEC, and beyond
by Mark Beeson (University of Birmingham)

Internet Governance (2009)
The new frontier of global institutions
by John Mathiason (Syracuse University)

The World Health Organization (2009)
by Kelley Lee (London School of Hygiene and Tropical Medicine)

International Judicial Institutions (2009)
The architecture of international justice at home and abroad
by Richard J. Goldstone (Retired Justice of the Constitutional Court of South Africa) and Adam M. Smith (Harvard University)

Institutions of the Global South (2009)
by Jacqueline Anne Braveboy-Wagner (City College of New York)

Global Food and Agricultural Institutions (2009)
by John Shaw

Shaping the Humanitarian World (2009)
by Peter Walker (Tufts University) and Daniel G. Maxwell (Tufts University)

The International Organization for Standardization and the Global Economy (2009)
Setting standards
by Craig N. Murphy (Wellesley College) and JoAnne Yates (Massachusetts Institute of Technology)

Organisation for Economic Co-operation and Development
by Richard Woodward (University of Hull)

Non-Governmental Organizations in Global Politics
by Peter Willetts (City University, London)

The International Labour Organization
by Steve Hughes (University of Newcastle) and Nigel Haworth (The University of Auckland Business School)

Global Institutions and the HIV/ AIDS Epidemic
Responding to an international crisis
by Franklyn Lisk (University of Warwick)

African Economic Institutions
by Kwame Akonor (Seton Hall University)

The United Nations Development Programme (UNDP)
by Elizabeth A. Mandeville (Tufts University) and Craig N. Murphy (Wellesley College)

The Regional Development Banks
Lending with a regional flavor
by Jonathan R. Strand (University of Nevada, Las Vegas)

Multilateral Cooperation Against Terrorism
by Peter Romaniuk (John Jay College of Criminal Justice, CUNY)

Transnational Organized Crime
by Frank Madsen (University of Cambridge)

Peacebuilding
From concept to commission
by Robert Jenkins (University of London)

Governing Climate Change
by Peter Newell (University of East Anglia) and Harriet A. Bulkeley (Durham University)

Millennium Development Goals (MDGs)
For a people-centered development agenda?
by Sakiko Fukada-Parr (The New School)

For further information regarding the series, please contact:

Craig Fowlie, Publisher, Politics & International Studies
Taylor & Francis
2 Park Square, Milton Park, Abingdon
Oxford OX14 4RN, UK

+44 (0)207 842 2057 Tel
+44 (0)207 842 2302 Fax

Craig.Fowlie@tandf.co.uk
www.routledge.com

Internet Governance
The new frontier of global institutions

John Mathiason

Routledge
Taylor & Francis Group

LONDON AND NEW YORK

First published 2009
by Routledge
2 Park Square, Milton Park, Abingdon, Oxon OX14 4RN

Simultaneously published in the USA and Canada
by Routledge
270 Madison Avenue, New York, NY 10016

Routledge is an imprint of the Taylor & Francis Group, an informa business

Typeset in Time New Roman by
Taylor & Francis Books
Printed and bound in Great Britain by
TJ International Ltd, Padstow, Cornwall

British Library Cataloguing in Publication Data
A catalogue record for this book is available from the British Library

Library of Congress Cataloging in Publication Data
Mathiason, John, 1942–
   Internet governance : the new frontier of global institutions / John
Mathiason.
      p. cm.—(Global institutions series)
   Includes bibliographical references and index.
   1. Internet—Government policy. I. Title.
   TK5105.875.
I57M3678 2008   384.3'3—dc22

ISBN 978-0-415-77402-4 (hbk)
ISBN 978-0-415-77403-1 (pbk)
ISBN 978-0-203-94608-4 (ebk)

Contents

List of illustrations   xi
Foreword   xiii
Acknowledgments   xvii
List of abbreviations   xviii

Introduction   1

1 What is the Internet and what is governance?   6

2 Before the Internet: communications and its regulation
   through history   24

3 The non-state actors: engineers, entrepreneurs, and
   netizens   32

4 Solving the domain name problem: Internet governance
   is born   49

5 Regulatory imperatives for Internet governance:
   downloading music, free speech, YouTube, porn, and
   crime and terrorism   59

6 The ICANN experiment   70

7 Multi-stakeholderism emerges from the World Summit
   on the Information Society   97

8 The IGF experiment begins   126

x *Contents*

9 What does the frontier look like?   146

   Notes   151
   Select bibliography   161
   Index   162

Illustrations

Figures

0.1	Internet domain survey host count	3
1.1	Internet packet formats	8
1.2	The Internet IP Postcard system	8
3.1	W3C accomplishments	41
6.1	Sources of revenue for ICANN, 2007–8	77
6.2	Structure of ICANN, October 2007	84
7.1	Participation by different entities in the Tunis summit Preparatory Committee meetings	123
8.1	IGF Athens meeting participation by stakeholder group	131

Tables

1.1	National and international policy issues in Internet governance	13
1.2	Organizational involvement by issue area	20
3.1	Chairs in the IETF, September 2007	36
3.2	Type of organization for IETF members by country of residence	37
3.3	Membership in the W3C, September 2007	39
3.4	Country of W3C member residency by type of organization	39
4.1	Original top-level domain names	50
4.2	Geographical distribution of original signers of the gTLD-MoU	53
4.3	Type of commenters by origin, March 1998	55
4.4	Orientation to international governance of the Internet, March 1998 comments	55

6.1   Initial members of the ICANN board of directors   75
6.2   Members of the ICANN board of directors, October
      2007   85
6.3   Composition of the Governmental Advisory Committee,
      by region, 1999–2004   89
7.1   Participants in Preparatory Committee 2, February
      2003, by type   105
7.2   Participants in Preparatory Committee 3, September
      2003, by type   110
7.3   Composition of the WGIG by type   118
8.1   Composition of the Multistakeholder Advisory
      Group (MAG) by constituency and region, May 2006   130
8.2   Structure of the Athens Forum, 2006   132
8.3   Structure of the Rio de Janeiro Forum, 2007   139

Boxes

1.1   Policy issues that needed to be addressed in Internet
      governance according to the Working Group on
      Internet Governance   19
6.1   Generic top-level domain names in force in October
      2007   94

Foreword

The current volume is the twenty-sixth in a dynamic series on "global institutions." The series strives (and, based on the volumes published to date, succeeds) to provide readers with definitive guides to the most visible aspects of what we know as "global governance." Remarkable as it may seem, there exist relatively few books that offer in-depth treatments of prominent global bodies, processes, and associated issues, much less an entire series of concise and complementary volumes. Those that do exist are either out of date, inaccessible to the non-specialist reader, or seek to develop a specialized understanding of particular aspects of an institution or process rather than offer an overall account of its functioning. Similarly, existing books have often been written in highly technical language or have been crafted "in-house" and are notoriously self-serving and narrow.

The advent of electronic media has helped by making information, documents, and resolutions of international organizations more widely available, but it has also complicated matters. The growing reliance on the Internet and other electronic methods of finding information about key international organizations and processes has served, ironically, to limit the educational materials to which most readers have ready access—namely, books. Public relations documents, raw data, and loosely refereed web sites do not make for intelligent analysis. Official publications compete with a vast amount of electronically available information, much of which is suspect because of its ideological or self-promoting slant. Paradoxically, the growing range of purportedly independent web sites offering analyses of the activities of particular organizations has emerged, but one inadvertent consequence has been to frustrate access to basic, authoritative, critical, and well-researched texts. The market for such has actually been reduced by the ready availability of varying quality electronic materials.

For those of us who teach, research, and practice in the area, this access to information has been particularly frustrating. We were delighted when Routledge saw the value of a series that bucks this trend and provides key reference points to the most significant global institutions. They know that serious students and professionals want serious analyses. We have assembled a first-rate line-up of authors to address that market. Our intention, then, is to provide one-stop shopping for all readers— students (both undergraduate and postgraduate), negotiators, diplomats, practitioners from nongovernmental and intergovernmental organizations, and interested parties alike—seeking information about the most prominent institutional aspects of global governance.

Internet governance

Governance and the Internet are two words that do not always sit comfortably together. The Internet's roots lie in the development of a communication apparatus that the U.S. military was keen to develop in the context of the bitter struggle with the Soviet Union during the Cold War. However, its champions celebrate its current status as a vehicle for freedom of expression, its unregulated quality, and its capacity to allow users access to information previously denied—a kind of global democratization of access for all. Although clearly wealthy countries have vastly better access than poor ones, that can be fixed. As the 2001 *Human Development Report* noted, "Policy, not charity, will determine whether new technologies become a tool for human development everywhere."[1]

For all of the protestations about who controls what, the Internet has always been subject to a modicum of governance. Its early designers created a medium of information and communication that gave rise to particular kinds of interaction and behavior. Its further evolution has been driven by the twin imperatives of access to information and commercial exploitation, both of which have shaped its development. National governments too have sought to exert their influence on the Internet's development, partially in response to the security challenges that it has thrown up and partially in response to pressure from commercial interests keen to ensure that they have a head start in the scramble for cyberspace.

In many respects, the governance of the Internet is an entirely new development for global governance—something that is to be expected given its novelty. Yet, for all its novelty, the regimes that are emerging to govern the Internet (regimes, because they are many and overlapping) are proceeding in a remarkably similar fashion to the development of governance regimes in other, much older, information and communication technologies. ICANN—the Internet Corporation for Assigned Names and Numbers—has evolved in strikingly similar ways to those world organizations that emerged to govern the flow of mail and telegrams across state boundaries in previous eras. While the context is different, the technologies the International Telegraph/Telecommunication Union (ITU) and the Universal Postal Union (UPU) sought to regulate in the middle of the nineteenth century were similarly revolutionary. And the pressures to extend them further—a desire to exploit their commercial potential coupled with the communications freedom they offered (not to mention their potential for military application)—are also remarkably alike.

Writing in the early 1990s—long before the shape of Internet governance had become anything near as clear as it has today (and there is still quite some way to go)—Craig Murphy described the role of such nineteenth-century international public unions in the following way:

> They have helped create international markets in industrial goods by linking *communication and transportation infrastructure*, protecting *intellectual property*, and reducing legal and economic barriers to *trade*. As a result, [these] world organizations have played a role in the periodic replacement of lead industries, a critical dynamic of the world economy since the Industrial Revolution.[2]

Murphy's insight resonates loudly with regard to the Internet. The technology might be new but the way in which the governance of the Internet is emerging, knitting together older forms of communication with those newer ones created by the "information superhighway,"[3] is comparable to the way in which the international public unions brought pre-existing forms of commerce and communication together with new and revolutionary techniques in the nineteenth century. Similarly, the Internet has enabled intellectual property right infringements to be more easily detected. And, it almost goes without saying that the Internet has been at the leading edge of industrial change across the globe.

Yet, while the manner in which Internet governance has proceeded has so far proven to be remarkably similar to the emergence of aspects of global governance in earlier epochs, the substance of that development still requires elucidation. Indeed, the technical details of the Internet and the complex manner in which it is governed are such that Internet governance is difficult to grasp.

We were delighted then when John Mathiason agreed to write this book. Indeed, there are few analysts who are better qualified than he to provide this *tour d'horizon* of what may be seen as the perfect symbol for a shrinking planet. John spent 25 years in a variety of spots within the United Nations, in the field and in headquarters, working on such issues as planning, the advancement of women, and rural development. Having earned his Ph.D. at the Massachusetts Institute of Technology, John was an unusual international civil servant in that he kept his hand in teaching and writing over the years, and has written about it.[4] Since the late-1990s, he has been an adjunct professor and senior research associate at Syracuse University's Maxwell School of Citizenship and Public Affairs.

It was during this time that he established his own consulting firm and put his own technical knowledge together with his passion for electronic communications. He has attended all of the preparatory and other planning sessions that have led to the current efforts to break the U.S. control of the Internet. This book and his own writings on the subject clearly tease out the pluses and minuses of the current ICANN regime.

John has produced a book that is brimming with information and authority, which could only be written by someone who has been present during recent international deliberations and who has keen analytical skills. As readers will quickly become aware, the book not only renders visible the tentative moves that have been made in governing the Internet, it also makes clear and readily accessible the complexities of the Internet itself. As such, the book is an invaluable resource. It clearly deserves to be read by all interested in the Internet and nascent forms of global governance. We heartily recommend it, and we welcome any comments that you may have.

Thomas G. Weiss, The CUNY Graduate Center, New York, USA
Rorden Wilkinson, University of Manchester, UK
July 2008

Acknowledgments

I gratefully acknowledge the assistance given to me by friends and colleagues. Uwe Gneiting, my research assistant at the Maxwell School, helped generate much of the data found in the tables. The comments by colleagues in the Internet Governance Project, including especially Milton Mueller and Jeanette Hofmann, have corrected errors of fact and interpretation. My spouse, Jan Clausen, contributed her usual admonition ("don't make it read like a UN document") as well as encouragement ("make it interesting, please"). The editors of the series, especially Tom Weiss, have ensured that it meets both stylistic and substantive standards. I am grateful to all of them.

Abbreviations

ALAC	At-Large Advisory Committee
APC	Association for Progressive Communication
ASO	Address Supporting Organization
BIRPPI	Bureaux Internationaux Réunis pour la Protection de la Propriété Intellectuelle (predecessor of the World Intellectual Property Organization)
CCITT	Telephone and Telegraph Consultative Committee
ccNSO	Country Code Names Supporting Organization
CERN	European Organization for Nuclear Research
CONGO	Conference of Non-Governmental Organizations in Consultative Status with the Economic and Social Council
CPSR	Computer Professionals for Social Responsibility
CSIF	Civil Society Internet Forum
DARPA	Defense Advanced Projects Administration
DNS	Domain Name System
DNSO	Domain Name Supporting Organization
DRM	Digital Rights Management
EFF	Electronic Frontier Foundation
GAC	Governmental Advisory Committee
GIGANET	Global Internet Governance Academic Network
GNSO	Generic Names Supporting Organization
GRULAC	Latin American and Caribbean Group of States
HTML	HyperText Markup Language
IAB	Internet Architecture Board
IANA	Internet Assigned Numbers Authority
ICANN	Internet Corporation for Assigned Names and Numbers
IEEE	Institute of Electrical and Electronics Engineers
IETF	Internet Engineering Task Force
IFWP	Internet Forum on the White Paper
IGF	Internet Governance Forum

IP	Internet Protocol
IPCC	Intergovernmental Panel on Climate Change
IPR	Intellectual Property Rights
ISO	International Organization for Standardization
ISP	Internet Service Provider
ITU	International Telecommunications Union
LAN	Local Area Network
MAG	Multistakeholder Advisory Group
NCUC	Non-Commercial Users Constituency
NGO	Non-Governmental Organization
NPA	National Planning Areas
NTIA	National Telecommunications and Information Administration
POTS	Plain Old Telephone Service
RATS	Rawalpindi Amateur Theatrical Society
RIAA	Recording Industry Association of America
SWITCH	Swiss Education and Research Network
TCP/IP	Transmission Control Protocol/Internet Protocol
TRIPS	Agreement on Trade-Related Aspects of Intellectual Property Rights
UDRP	Uniform Dispute Resolution Process
UNDP	United Nations Development Programme
UNESCO	United Nations Educational, Scientific and Cultural Organization
UNICT	United Nations Information and Communications Technology Task Force
UPU	Universal Postal Union
W3C	World Wide Web Consortium
WGIG	Working Group on Internet Governance
WIPO	World Intellectual Property Organization
WSIS	World Summit on the Information Society
WTO	World Trade Organization

Introduction

On 30 June 2006, Ted Stevens, U.S. senator from Alaska, stated in a Senate hearing on an amendment inserting some very basic net neutrality provisions into a moving telecommunications bill:[1]

> I just the other day got, an internet was sent by my staff at 10 o'clock in the morning on Friday and I just got it yesterday. Why?
>
> Because it got tangled up with all these things going on the internet commercially.
>
> So you want to talk about the consumer? Let's talk about you and me. We use this internet to communicate and we aren't using it for commercial purposes.
>
> We aren't earning anything by going on that internet. Now I'm not saying you have to or you want to discriminate against those people.
>
> The regulatory approach is wrong. Your approach is regulatory in the sense that it says "No one can charge anyone for massively invading this world of the internet." No, I'm not finished. I want people to understand my position, I'm not going to take a lot of time.
>
> They want to deliver vast amounts of information over the internet. And again, the internet is not something you just dump something on. It's not a truck.
>
> It's a series of tubes.
>
> And if you don't understand those tubes can be filled and if they are filled, when you put your message in, it gets in line and it's going to be delayed by anyone that puts into that tube enormous amounts of material, enormous amounts of material.
>
> ...
>
> Now I think these people are arguing whether they should be able to dump all that stuff on the internet ought to consider if they should develop a system themselves.

Senator Stevens' statement was greeted with great hilarity by persons knowledgeable about the Internet and was attributed to his age (76), which presumably limited his understanding of the new communications means that most high school students (or younger) already dominate. But none-the-less there was a certain amount of insight in the senator's statement.

The Internet is not a truck. The senator was right about that. And it really is not a series of tubes, either, although he is only partly wrong about that. The Internet is a complex communications system that, among other things, has pipes—as the fiber-optic cables that are the main channels for messages are called.

And, when the senator said "the regulatory approach is wrong" he pointed to a problem that regulation is being imposed on the Internet and the real question is what regulatory approach is right.

This book is about how governments, the private sector, intergovernmental organizations, civil society and the academic and technical community are trying to agree on how to regulate—or govern—the Internet. It shows the evolution of their different approaches leading to a new form of multi-stakeholder governance that may change not only how the Internet is governed but also how other problems that transcend national borders can be solved. It is about a new frontier for global governance, being worked out in a specific context.

At the beginning of the twenty-first century, the Internet as a means of communication is ubiquitous and powerful. In the twenty-five years since 1983 when it began its meteoric growth,[2] its users expanded from a few million technologically adept people to the billion or so that use it regularly in 2007 with over half a billion registered domain servers (see Figure 0.1).

Tony Rutkowski, the first executive director of the Internet Society said: "internetworking is one of the most revolutionary technologies of the twentieth century ... indeed it may perhaps be the most revolutionary human communications medium that has ever emerged."[3] The Internet's pervasiveness is changing politics, economics and social relations. Its borderless nature affects the roles of individuals, the magic of the marketplace and the problems of government regulation. As its development has increased apace, contradictions have arisen between existing regulatory regimes, private interests, government concerns, international norms and national interests. Unlike most areas where global institutions have been created, where the role of governments is predominant, the Internet is a field where the private sector and civil society each have a role as important—or sometimes more important—than governments. The borderless nature of the Internet (recognized by

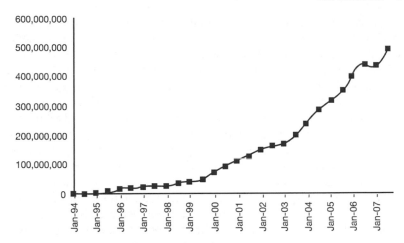

Figure 0.1 Internet domain survey host count.
Source: Internet Systems Consortium (www.isc.org).

most analysts) produces particular needs for global institutions and has opened the door for innovative approaches.

The Internet began in a scientific and technical environment in which governments were absent, except as a funding source. The issue of Internet governance began around a technical issue with economic consequences, the scarcity of domain names which are key elements in the addressing system, and, after a domestic process in the United States, led to the creation of the Internet Corporation for Assigned Names and Numbers (ICANN), a private entity under government supervision but with a governance model that tried to involve governments, the private sector and individual users. This became controversial itself, and critics began to question how the ICANN was evolving.

The larger governance issue emerged during the first half of the World Summit on the Information Society (WSIS) in December 2003, where questions were raised about unilateral oversight of the Internet by a single government. This opened the door to other issues, and Internet governance became the main concern of the second half of WSIS. A Working Group on Internet Governance (WGIG) that was multi-stakeholder in composition guided preparations for the final WSIS in Tunis in November 2005. The follow-up to WSIS was a new form of international institution: a multi-stakeholder forum that, without decision-making authority, would constrain and guide governmental decision-making, consistent with the insights of international regime theory. The first meeting of the forum in Athens in November 2006 began a process where this new institution will eventually serve to define a new approach to global governance that is based on a relative equality of stakeholders, even within the Westphalian system of states.

The book tells the story of this new frontier, where the linkage between technology, information, individuals, old regulatory regimes and new approaches has led to a great experiment, which a volume produced by the United Nations Information and Communications Technology Task Force called "A Grand Collaboration."[4] Like any good story, the book starts in Chapter 1 with a description of the context by filling out Senator Stevens' description of what the Internet is. It then introduces the cast of characters, starting with governments and international organizations (Chapter 2) and then introducing the many non-state actors involved (Chapter 3). It dwells on the technical issue that triggered the Internet governance debate (Chapter 4) and its larger implications (Chapter 5), and then follows the evolution of institutions to today, starting with ICANN (Chapter 6), then the World Summit on the Information Society (Chapter 7) and concluding with the Internet Governance Forum (Chapter 8). Finally, it draws some conclusions about the application of the multi-stakeholder process for other issue areas (Chapter 9).

Together with my collaborators on the Internet Governance Project— a group of scholars located at Syracuse University and Georgia Tech in the United States and the Technical University of Berlin in Europe—I have been part of the evolutionary story of the Internet. I began writing on Internet governance at the time of the original domain name controversy, arguing that the internationalization of the Internet would need principles, norms and procedures if the Internet was to grow successfully.[5] At the time, this was not a popular position and, while maintaining a watching brief, I went on to other concerns. In the interim, the Internet bubble was created in the U.S. economy just as the Internet became ubiquitous, the United States after invading Iraq became suspect in multilateral circles, and increasingly governments wanted to regulate the Internet.

Then, in November 2003, Internet governance emerged from the first part of the World Summit on the Information Society as a main issue and what was supposed to be a technical conference became very political. The internationalization of the Internet had, as I would have predicted, become a matter of concern to all stakeholders including governments, the private sector, civil society and even academia. The immediate focus of controversy was the addressing mechanism maintained by ICANN, which had been intensively examined by my IGP colleague Milton Mueller.[6] When the United Nations Information and

Communications Technology Task Force organized a forum on Internet governance in April 2004, Milton and I, together with our colleagues Lee McBride, Hans Klein and Marc Holitscher prepared an analysis of what we called "the state of play" that showed how many of the existing international regimes and institutions were affected by the Internet governance issue.[7] We organized the Internet Governance Project as an institutional vehicle to provide an academic look at the issue and over the last several years we have published a number of papers on the issues of the moment.[8]

The second half of the World Summit held in Tunis in November 2005 agreed that the issue of Internet governance needed to be addressed but decided that the venue would be a non-binding, innovative and rather amorphous multi-stakeholder Internet Governance Forum (IGF). This was a compromise between those countries that wanted no international mechanism to deal with the Internet and those that wanted a formal structure. The IGF held its first meeting in Athens in October 2006. Even after the first meeting, the form and structure has been evolving. At the same time, an existing body, the United Nations Commission on Science and Technology for Development was, to the surprise of its members, given the responsibility of following up WSIS, including Internet Governance. The second meeting of the IGF took place in Rio de Janeiro in November 2007, and the structure evolved further.

Creating a viable institutional structure that will protect the Internet as an open communications medium but with realistic economic and political constraints is still a work in progress. This book, then, is an interim brief, but one that should give the reader the tools to understand what happens next as the institution evolves.

1 What is the Internet and what is governance?

The chapter introduces the concept of the Internet as it has emerged, based on technology and how it might be defined. It then looks at what governance, as contrasted with government, would mean, again in current usage.

To be able to discuss Internet governance, we need to know what each term means. This is a significant question, because although the WSIS defined "Internet governance," there is no agreed definition of what the Internet is, nor what governance implies. When the Internet is defined, the aspects that can be regulated can also be defined. When governance is defined, the limits of regulation will also be set out.

In communication theory, a communication consists of five parts: a sender, a message, a channel, a receiver and a feedback mechanism. At its simplest, for a traditional telephone conversation to take place, you (the sender) have a telephone into which you speak (the message) that carries your voice over either a fixed line or wireless (the channel) to the phone of another person (the receiver) who can reply (feedback). Of course, it is more complex than that. Your telephone has to be connected to a network that is run by a telephone company through either wires into your home or office or through a wireless transmission tower. That network has to be connected to the network that your receiver is on. Often the receiver's network is supplied by a different company. It could even be a company in a different country, in which case there would have to be international standards to permit the call to go through. This would include such issues as the technical standards (which kinds of telephone numbers would be allowed) and financial arrangements (since the cost of the call is charged to the sender, how is the company providing services to the receiver of the call going to collect for its services). Internet mavens refer to this process as Plain Old Telephone Service (POTS).

Communication over the Internet is similar to POTS, but different in critical ways. It is a network of networks (which is where the term Internet comes from). There are senders (anyone using a computer to connect with the network), there are messages, in the form of e-mails or requests for information, there are channels including those made available by companies or institutions like universities—called Internet service providers (or ISPs) that connect the individual to the larger network of networks. There are channels, usually large fiber-optic cables called pipes, over which messages flow and there are recipients who are connected to the Internet though their own ISPs.

Here the similarities end. Unlike POTS, the Internet is borderless.

What is the Internet?

Although telephone switching systems have matured to the point that hundreds of millions of connections a day can be set up and maintained by the network, their essential characteristic remains a continuous full-time pathway between two points at any one time.[1]

The Internet is based on a technology called packet switching. Packet switching represents a significantly different communications model. It is based on the ability to place content in digital form, which simply means that content can be coded into binary numbers (1 or 0), which is how computers store information. In packet switching, the content of communication, once put into digital form, is divided into small, well defined groups of coded data, each with an identifying numerical address. Anything that can be digitized can be sent as a packet. To the Internet, a packet is a packet is a packet, whether it carries numbers, words, digitized sounds or digitized pictures. It became possible, and the U.S. Defense Department's Arpanet actualized the possibility (see Chapter 3), to send an unlimited number of packets over the same circuit with different addresses. Routers, rather than switches, became the key to delivering the packets to the intended destination. Figure 1.1 shows the packet format.[2]

Controlled by software and microprocessors, the router inspects the address of a packet and sends it on its way on a full-time circuit to another router to an eventual end point. As the network technology evolved into the TCP/IP network that undergirds the Internet, the designers reserved 32 bits for the packet address (to be superseded by 128 bits in Internet Protocol version 6 [Ipv6]) which are represented in decimal notation in a format xxx.xxx.xxx.xxx, where each group of x's can range from 0 to 255. Figure 1.2 shows how the packets are routed.

The Internet Protocol, an agreement on a standard for setting up packets, is one key part of the Internet. A second key part is the addressing system, the management of which was the first governance issue.

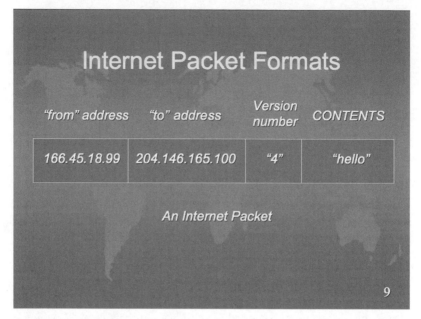

Figure 1.1 Internet packet formats.

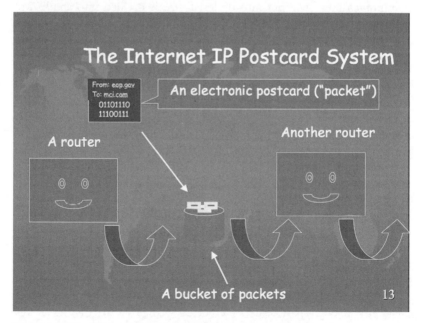

Figure 1.2 The Internet IP Postcard system.

The innovation of a Domain Name System (DNS) in 1984, prior to the creation of the Web in 1988–89, provided synonyms for the somewhat inscrutable digit strings of the actual address. The actual addresses of the packets remained the digit strings but they were replaceable by more or less scrutable alphabetic equivalents stored on a DNS server file which permitted the lookup of the alphabetic name from a numerical address and vice versa. Thus was born the web site name, a new entity and a new property right in a new and legally ambiguous sphere.

By comparison, the telephone system addressing system started in the simplest possible fashion with Sally asking an operator to connect her to Harry. Under the direction of the Bell System-affiliated companies and by agreement with the non-Bell operating companies, the present U.S. ten-digit area code–exchange–line number system evolved over decades into a national standard. By contrast, the Internet addressing scheme was designed from its day of creation by engineers and scientists as a logical and comprehensive construct to meet their needs for low-cost data communication. The integrity of the scheme was guaranteed by its sponsorship by the U.S. Department of Defense and by later private sector successors.

The alphabetic names associated with numeric addresses were divided into domains, a limited typology of alpha addresses that enabled the routers to do their lookups efficiently. To find the numeric twin of the Internet address of "UN.ORG," for instance, the router need not search through every entry in its address table, just the addresses ending in ".ORG." These suffixes as the first level of searching and selecting are known as top level domains: the original set included .COM, .MIL, .ORG, .GOV and .NET, corresponding to net addresses for entities in commercial, military, non-profit, government and network administration endeavors.

Internet addresses are conceptually very different from telephone numbers. In the U.S.A., Canada and the Caribbean, most area codes (technically NPAs—National Planning Areas) denote a geographic place with boundaries identifiable with governmental jurisdictions: nations, states, cities. The exchange part of the phone number is traditionally associated with a specific place with a street address, the central office, from which the wires emerge to connect the telephone user over the "last mile" to the network. The place-centered nature of the phone system numbering plan is beginning to break down with the rise of wireless cellular systems, the widespread use of ghostly 800 and 888 numbers which may be answered here one minute and there the next. Nonetheless, jurisdiction can be established in all cases. Internationally, the country code, city code numbering system links phone number to place to the jurisdiction.

Internet addresses have no fixed location. They are purely conceptual. There is no central office. The routers which direct packets to the packet address at rates between 100,000 and 500,000 a second can know only the next logical point in a routing table and which outbound circuit is available to carry the packet. Packets are free to traverse the globe on countless circuits to geographically indeterminate end points. The technology provides assurance that the packets are reassembled in the right order and are very likely not corrupted by data errors.

A further distinguishing factor in net addresses is that neither the sender nor the receiver of a packet is a paying customer for the packet. Telephony requires two paying customers to complete a call, each of whom is paying for the privilege and each of whom has at a minimum a billing address and usually a street address in a city, a state/province and country. The Internet senders and receivers are inherently tied neither by the billing process, since they do not pay for the specific message nor the technology to place the message, since the packets can go by various channels.

The technical underpinnings of novel realities have led to major policy debates that are far from resolved. From inside the Internet, names for addresses are structured but purely arbitrary, the technology is indifferent to content, and the sender/receiver dyad is unlocatable in a conventional spatial sense.

The packets containing content are coded in the sender's computer by e-mail programs, or by web-authoring programs. The computer is then connected to a local network by the Internet Service Provider through what are called servers—computers that have software to store and route data. In my case, when I am working from home, my computer is connected to Syracuse University's computer facilities by my telephone company (although it could also be by my television cable company or even my electrical utility). The ISP's routers send the packets toward the address that is their destination (and if the address is wrong, will send an error message). Usually this will be over the large fiber-optic cable networks called "pipes" that are owned by private companies. The packets will follow a path of least resistance and not all packets will follow the same path. This is one reason that the Internet is so efficient. Eventually (and this can be a very fast eventually since the packets go at approximately the speed of light), the packets arrive at the server managing the receiver's address. In my case, e-mails sent to me at my Syracuse University address (syr.edu) will arrive at my mailbox, be joined together into a single message and I will be able to download them to my own computer and read the content.

How fast the content gets to me depends on a couple of factors. It depends on the speed of my computer, which has to decode the digital files into something I can read (through application software like Apple Mail, Microsoft Mail or the open source Mozilla Thunderbird for e-mail, or a web browser software like Mozilla Firefox, Safari, Internet Explorer or Netscape). It also depends on the speed of my connection to my ISP. If I am at the University, I can connect via an Ethernet Local Area Network (LAN), if I am at home, it is via a tele-phone fiber-optic cable or a coaxial cable from the television cable company. The speed with which packets can be sent over these lines is called "bandwidth."

Some content like e-mail requires very little bandwidth, because the number of packets is small. Other content, like digitalized movies, has massive numbers of packets and takes a long time to download. The content that a person can obtain depends in large measure on the bandwidth available and as the Internet has matured, this has increased.

So, what can we say that the Internet is? As can be seen, the simple question has a complicated answer. We can say simply that it is a communication channel or medium and as such a piece of the com-munication process. It is a network of networks, starting with the net-work of which a sender is a part, continuing to larger networks that link smaller ones, and finishing with the network of which the receiver is part. The networks connect because of agreed protocols. Most of these are technical pieces of engineering software that are agreed by technicians. As institutions, the Internet is made up of individuals who get services from institutions (companies, universities, government offices) who get services from other institutions who may invest in infrastructure or technological development.

In seeking to provide a useful definition, Milton Mueller, Hans Klein and I proposed a concise definition of the Internet:[3]

> The Internet is the global data communication capability realized by the interconnection of public and private telecommunication networks using Internet Protocol (IP), Transmission Control Protocol (TCP), and the other protocols required to implement IP inter-networking on a global scale, such as DNS and packet routing protocols.

For most things, the Internet operates automatically. Once you have written an e-mail and given the address of the recipient, the rest is taken care of by the protocols and the machines they run on.

So why do we worry about governance of this system? If we didn't have to worry about either the content of messages being sent over the system, or the cost of running or joining the Internet, only a very simple form of management would be needed. There would only have to be a mechanism to agree on the protocols that make the networks link to each other and there would have to be some means of maintaining order in the addressing system. In fact, as we will see in more detail in Chapter 3, this was how the Internet was originally run. A group of engineers and scientists would get together periodically through an ad hoc body that called itself the Internet Engineering Task Force (IETF) to agree on the content of protocols. One individual, Professor Jon Postel of the computer center at the University of Southern California, ran a directory that contained all of the addresses being used.

This ideal state only lasted a very short time, because a large number of policy issues intruded on the Internet, many of which did not directly relate to the engineering architecture of the system, but all of which were either causes or consequences of issues with the technology.

One way to look at policy is to use the component parts of communication: (a) a sender, (b) a message, (c) a channel or medium, (d) a receiver, and (e) feedback. Each component has its own policy issues and stakeholders. Table 1.1 shows some of these issues, both at the national and international levels and the stakeholders concerned with them.

It is no coincidence that the first two universal international organizations were concerned with communications: the Universal Postal Union and what was then named the International Telegraph Union (see Chapter 2 for details). Without some regulatory mechanism, communication flows over national borders could not be assured. Both institutions have endured (with the ITU renamed the International Telecommunications Union) as what are now termed technical agencies of the United Nations system. The ITU has continued to be involved with the Internet.

The question is, however, will the Internet change the parameters of international policy—including regulation; can the existing agencies perform the task; and is there now a need for a conscious international communications policy?

The sender

The key issue for senders is to ensure access. In order to be a sender, one needs a method of identification. The need for order in identification

Table 1.1 National and international policy issues in Internet governance

Communication aspect	National issue	International efforts	Stakeholders
Sender	Universal service Nondiscrimination Competition Trademarks Tax policy	Developing country access (UNDP/World Bank/ITU) Nondiscrimination (UNHCHR) Competition in services (WTO) Authentication (UNCITRAL) Domain name registration (ITU/WIPO) Trademarks (WIPO)	E-commerce companies Software producers Electronic media Universities and libraries Netizens
Message	Content regulation Copyright	Norms for content regulation (UNHCHR) Copyright (WIPO)	Government censors Press, film, music industry Civil libertarians
Medium	Telecom regulation Encryption policy Competition Public investment	Transmission standards and protocols (ITU) Satellite orbit slots (ITU) Competition (WTO) Payments policy (ITU) Infrastructure investment (World Bank)	Telecommunications companie Banks and financial service companies Internet service providers
Receiver	Universal access	Universal access	User groups Students and researchers
Feedback	Access to governance Interactivity Finance	Access to governance Interactivity	Non-governmental organizations Industry groups Developing country governments

is reflected in the discussions about how best to register domain names. In that sense, it is probably not surprising that the first large controversy in international regulation was in that area. Here the market mechanism has largely failed, since only a regulatory decision solved the problem of who would be registrars. The controversy also lays out in stark relief that there are many more significant parties to the question than just governments: individual and corporate senders, non-governmental organizations, channel providers and receivers as well.

A second issue for senders is the freedom to send messages. This is partly a matter of content (as will be seen below) but is also a matter of having a network on which any sender can expect to reach receivers

Here the question turns on whether reasonable access can be obtained to Internet service providers, with minimal regulation and reasonable cost, and whether receivers can be expected to be able to get the messages. This latter, again, is a matter of provision of the appropriate technology at a reasonable cost.

Cost is related to the degree of competition among senders, and here the work of the World Trade Organization in terms of increasing trade in services is relevant.

Organizations of senders are beginning to develop. These can be nationally based, as many are, but they are increasingly transnational. This in itself is a new phenomenon. It creates the prospect of international non-governmental organizations of senders that need not be comprised, as are traditional NGOs, of federations of national affiliates.

The message

Issues of message relate to regulation of content. What messages should be allowed, who will determine whether they will be allowed and who will regulate this? The Internet developed as an almost free market for ideas, but many individuals and a few national authorities have found messages objectionable. An example is the efforts at censorship of adult material by the German government through prosecution of CompuServe managers for alleged pornographic content. A similar issue can be said to have been raised by efforts to regulate the use of encryption technology.

Communications policy includes regulatory policy, and there are already efforts to develop national regulatory norms that would be applicable to the Internet, most recently the German Information and Communication Services Bill. These are highly controversial, since restriction in one kind of content may set precedents for wider regulation. They also pose national constitutional questions, as was found in the case of the invalidation of the Communications Decency Law in the United States by the Supreme Court. They are also likely to be ineffective, since the borderless nature of the Internet makes applicability of national regulations highly problematic.

The medium

The medium or channel over which the message is sent has historically been the focus of communications regulation. Partly this was because the channel, which was a physical entity, could be regulated. Partly it was because communications channels, like frequencies or lines that passed over public lands, were inherently public goods. At the international level this aspect of regulation has been reflected in international standards for bandwidths, frequency allocations and exchange protocols. It has also been reflected in agreements on the allocation of geostationary orbit slots

Ensuring competition among providers of media has been a concern. Just as many governments are privatizing their national telecommunications systems, mergers among main Internet pipe providers have raised the specter of monopoly and have produced some efforts at regulation, as is the case of European Commission scrutiny of the MCI/WorldCom merger in 1998.

A new effort at regulation through the medium is found in an increasing effort to regulate content by regulating channel providers. These include the cases of the government of Austria shutting down an Internet service provider by confiscating its physical servers, or a libel action against America On-line, as well as the previously mentioned German case. The futility of this type of regulation has also been demonstrated.

Perhaps more importantly, telecommunications technology is increasingly intersecting with the recognized global commons, as satellite-based transmission technologies designed to increase bandwidth and ensure coverage begin to compete for scarce orbital slots. The fact that two private corporations, Teldesic and a consortium of Motorola and others, at one point intended to place a large number of communications satellites in orbit would inevitably require some effort at regulation. Similarly, the increase of wireless transmission is already leading to regulatory efforts on a national basis and can be expected increasingly to enter international "space."

The receiver

As in the case of senders, the key issue for receivers of messages is access. One should be able to receive the messages that one wishes and the Internet, with its packet delivery technology, facilitates this.

Access, however, can be controlled by cost, by regulation or by technology (e.g. v-chips, surf watchers). The largest obstacle, however, is access to service providers, particularly in the developing countries. Partly this is a matter of technology transfer, partly of cost. However, as events such as the World Bank/UNDP/Canada Global Knowledge '97 Conference showed, many of the technical solutions are available, if they can be disseminated.

The real question is cost, including those of national telecommunications. Here it is partly a matter of local assignment of costs, which is related to telecommunications monopolies and the issue of competition, partly it is a matter of how international prices are calculated. In the matter of postal rates, which may have an analogy with Internet rates, mechanisms have been put in place to adjust rates to both national and international reality in the public interest.

Feedback

The final aspect of communications is feedback. Here the interactive nature of the Internet makes it perhaps the most complete communications system yet devised. How and whether feedback can be regulated is as yet an open question, although well publicized libel cases against Matt Droan and America On-Line indicate that there is an issue here. Similarly, the role of gatekeepers, including non-governmental organizations, in channeling feedback has yet to be explored.

Each of the elements also involves its stakeholders whose interests may conflict.

At the national level, political processes and governments address these issues, but what happens at the international level? Here we have to look at something different, called "governance."

What does governance mean?

Don MacLean, a Canadian expert on the Internet, found a very usable definition for governance.[4] He wrote:

> In the English language, "governance" is an old term which, like "civil society," fell into disuse, but which has been revived, given new meaning, and attained widespread currency. Like "government" and "governor," it is derived from the Latin word "gubernare"— the action of steering a ship. A popular definition reflects these ancient Roman roots by defining governance as "steering, not rowing."

This difference was recognized by international relations theorists who developed the concept of international regimes. The consensus definition of international regimes is "sets of implicit or explicit principles, norms, rules, and decision-making procedures around which actors' expectations converge in a given area of international relations."[5] What this says is that order is maintained in a given area because all of the stakeholders concerned are convinced that order is necessary and agree on what should be done to maintain it. Because there is no coercive force to obligate compliance, it is governance (steering) rather than government (rowing) in the terms used by Maclean. The borderless, multistakeholder nature of the Internet means that it can be "governanced" but not governed.

Regime theory further defines what has to be agreed. This includes principles, norms, rules, and decision-making procedures. "Principles are beliefs of fact, causation, and rectitude. Norms are standards of behavior defined in terms of rights and obligations. Rules are specific prescriptions or proscriptions for action. Decision-making procedures are prevailing practices for making and implementing collective choice."[6]

Many international regimes have been created or are in the process of creation. Often they are managed by international organizations and are structured around international conventions—multilateral treaties that create legally binding obligations for governments. Many of these are relevant for Internet governance and overlap, causing potential conflicts.

In an analysis prepared for the UNICT Task Force in 2004, I, together with Milton Mueller, Hans Klein and Lee McKnight distinguished three governance functions:[7]

Technical Standardization: This involves decisions about the basic networking protocols, software applications, and data formats (e.g. Internet protocol versions 4 and 6).

Resource Allocation and Assignment: Some elements of the Internet are scarce or require exclusive use and their distribution to users must be coordinated (e.g. domain names and IP address numbers). This function also includes operational responsibilities connected to resource assignment, such as DNS root server management.

Public Policy: The third governance function is policy formulation, policy enforcement and dispute resolution. Whereas the previous two governance functions concern technology, public policy governs the *conduct* of people and organizations. Consistent with the technology-based definition of Internet governance, this function refers only to people and organizations directly involved in the design, operation, or use of the services and networks employing the Internet protocols.

Table 1.2 shows which organizations are involved in different issue areas. Organizations are classified by type, and activities are coded by governance function.

A large number of organizations, both state and non-state, are actively involved in Internet governance. The actors performing the first two governance functions—standardization and resource allocation and assignment—are mostly non-state actors. The actors performing the third type of governance functions—public policy—are mostly state actors. Among state actors there is a clear segmentation of organizations by issue area. In the areas of commerce and intellectual property, states have had to confront the implications of the Internet for pre-existing agreements, but the range of issues is clearly growing as these implications are becoming clearer. Some non-state actors play significant roles here. Most notable is ICANN, whose policy activities span several issue areas (discussed in Chapter 5).

The governance problem is to ensure that the functions, and the actors who perform them, as a whole provide enough order for the Internet to work.

What is Internet governance?

When the issue of Internet governance was raised at the Geneva segment of the World Summit on the Information Society in 2003, the Plan of Action that was adopted by governments asked the secretary-general of the United Nations to set up a working group on Internet governance that would, among other things, "develop a working definition of Internet governance."[8]

The Working Group on Internet Governance (WGIG), as described in Chapter 7, was duly constituted, met and recommended a working definition that was duly incorporated into the Tunis Agenda. The definition of Internet governance is "the development and application by governments, the private sector and civil society, in their respective roles, of shared principles, norms, rules, decision-making procedures, and programmes that shape the evolution and use of the Internet."[9]

The WGIG proposed a number of policy issues that needed to be addressed in Internet governance.[10] Box 1.1 shows these included (within the three-part structure proposed by Mathiason, Mueller, Klein, and McKnight).

> **Box 1.1 Policy issues that needed to be addressed in Internet governance according to the Working Group on Internet Governance**
>
> - Administration of the root zone files and system (Resource Allocation and Assignment)
> - Interconnection costs (Resource Allocation and Assignment)
> - Internet stability, security and cybercrime (Public Policy)
> - Spam (Public Policy)
> - Meaningful participation in global policy development (Public Policy)
> - Capacity-building (Public Policy)
> - Allocation of domain names (Resource Allocation and Assignment)
> - IP addressing (Technical Standardization)
> - Intellectual property rights (IPR) (Public Policy)
> - Freedom of expression (Public Policy)
> - Data protection and privacy rights (Public Policy)
> - Consumer rights (Public Policy)
> - Multilingualism (Public Policy)
> - Others, including
>   - convergence and "next generation networks" (NGNs) (Technical Standardization);
>   - trade and ecommerce (Public Policy).

The range of issues is very wide indeed, but most are in the governance domain of public policy. We will find these issues recurring throughout our exploration.

Who should govern?

While it might seem that governments should run the Internet, in reality there are five groups of stakeholders in governance, and the debate on governance turns on the role for each. The five are:

1 Individual governments reflecting national interests;
2 International organizations, reflecting the views of their inter-governmental bodies and their secretariats;
3 The private sector, consisting of corporations—mostly multinational—working as individuals or through their associations such as the International Chamber of Commerce;

Table 1.2 Organizational involvement by issue area

Issue Area	Issue	State (Intergovernmental) Universal			
		ITU	WIPO	UN HCHR UNESCO	WTO
Human rights	Privacy			Human rights conventions	
	Content			Optional Protocol to CRC; CERD TLD strings ICRA, PICs Content UNESCO promotion of knowledge, culture Commission	
	Freedom of expression		UDRP – critical domain names	Human Rights CCPR	
IPR	Copyright		1996 Performance Phono Treaty; 1996 Copyright Treaty		TRIPS
	Trademark		UDRP; 2nd domain name proceeding; 2001 Joint Rec on Marks UDRP		
	Patents		IPR Patents Substantive Patent Law Treaty		
International economic relations	Trade				TRIPS
	E-commerce				
	Consumer protection				
	Taxation				Policy discussion
	Competition policy				
Enforcement of order	Network and IS security	Plenipot Resolution 130			
	Cyber crime and cyber terrorism				
	Spam	Meetings			
	Authentication and identity	PKI standards			
Operational policies for the Internet	Global resource management	E.164 ccTLD meetings ENUM cc's, .int			
	Interconnection	ICAIS, Rec. D.50 IP-PSTN interop			

Technical standardization   Resource assignment   Policy development, rules, recommendations

Universal		Non-universal			
UNCITRAL	*UN-ODC*	*EU CoE*	*OECD*	*APEC-ASEAN*	*Hague Conference G8*
		EU 1995 Directive	Guidelines		Lyon Group 2001 recommendations
		CoE Declaration		1999 ASEAN porn framework	

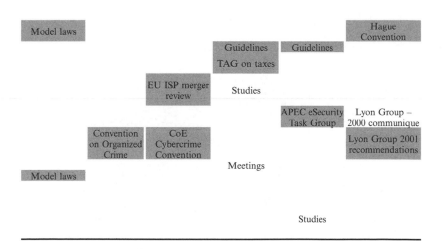

Model laws					Hague Convention
			Guidelines TAG on taxes	Guidelines	
		EU ISP merger review	Studies		
				APEC eSecurity Task Group	Lyon Group – 2000 communique
	Convention on Organized Crime	CoE Cybercrime Convention			Lyon Group 2001 recommendations
Model laws			Meetings		
				Studies	

Table continued on next page.

Table 1.2 continued

| Issue Area | Issue | Non-state | | | | |
| | | Formal | | | Informal | |
		ICANN	ISC	RIRs	IETF	Others
Human rights	Privacy	Whois Database policy			IRIS	
	Content	TLD strings				ICRA, PICs W3C accessibility standards
IPR	Freedom of expression Copyright	UDRP – critical domain names				
	Trademark	UDRP				
	Patents					
International economic relations	Trade E-commerce Consumer protection Taxation					
	Competition policy	TLD creation Registry Contracts Registrar Accred.				
Enforcement of order	Network and IS security	SSAC			Routing security	DNSSEC Secure BGP
	Cyber crime and cyber terrorism		BIND			
	Spam					ASTA Studies
	Authentication and identity	Whois data accuracy		IP address Whois		
Operational policies for the Internet	Global resource management	IP address DNS Root	anycast RSs BIND	ENUM root (RIPE) IP address	IDN standards	
	Interconnection				Routing protocols	

4 Non-governmental organizations, consisting of representatives of different constituencies, working through groupings like the Conference of NGOs or the Civil Society Caucus, as well as individual organizations like the Electronic Frontier Foundation, and Computer Professionals for Social Responsibility;

5 Academics, consisting mostly of individual scholars, working through such groupings as the Global Internet Governance Academic Network (GIGANET), the Internet Governance Project or the Diplo Foundation.

These stakeholders are reflected in different ways in the different institutions that are emerging to deal with Internet governance and will be seen throughout the analysis. In looking at how these stakeholders interact, however, we should be mindful of something said by Bruce Sterling, referring to a law enforcement group in the United States in his book on prosecution of hackers:[11]

> For years now, economists and management theorists have speculated that the tidal wave of the information revolution would destroy rigid, pyramidal bureaucracies, where everything is top-down and centrally controlled. Highly trained "employees" would take on much greater autonomy, being self-starting, and self-motivating, moving from place to place, task to task, with great speed and fluidity. "Ad-hocracy" would rule, with groups of people spontaneously knitting together across organizational lines, tackling the problem at hand, applying intense computer-aided expertise to it, and then vanishing whence they came.

We now have some sense of what the Internet is and some sense of what governance at the international level implies. We still must determine, in practice, what the combined term means.

2 Before the Internet
Communications and its regulation through history

Before the Internet dominated the global communications system, there had been regulation by international organizations to ensure order in telecommunications and in intellectual property. While the Internet's borderless nature has rendered that old system ineffective, understanding how and why the old system was created can demonstrate why Internet governance is important now.

Communications was one of the first activities to have international regulation. For communications to cross borders, standards were needed and the economics of transnational commerce required agreements. Both were reflected in what is widely considered to be the first universal international organization, the International Telegraph Union (ITU). Then, property transmitted over communications channels also needed to be regulated. But before the Internet the processes, while technically complex, were conceptually simple.

The channel: the early history of international organizations

Although Samuel F. B. Morse had invented the telegraph in 1844, its initial progress was slow because telegraph lines did not run over national boundaries. Each country had different standards and to make the system work smoothly, many countries, especially in Europe, decided to create formal arrangements to facilitate interconnection. The countries decided to standardize equipment, initially by a large number of bilateral and regional agreements.[1]

The futility of trying to work out arrangements bilaterally, which had been the method used for most of previous history, was clear in this case. Unless there was an agreement on transmission standards, there would be no messages. Similarly, transborder communication raised issues of payment and compensation. While goods could be traded across borders based on negotiated prices and tariffs applied at the borders, information had to be paid for at either one end of the communication link or the other. While it would have been possible to collect fees from the sender, as a condition for putting a message into the system, and then collect fees from the receiver, as a condition for getting the message out of the system, this would be unwieldy, difficult technically and would have probably killed the method.

The compromise was to collect fees only at one end—the sender— and then share the fees with the service that provided the message to the receiver. These are what are now called interconnection costs. How much to share has to be negotiated and agreed.

The initial treaty was only among continental European countries,[2] reflecting the importance of physical proximity for telegraph lines. The initial treaty dealt with principles and norms, including ensuring that messages are transmitted freely. They agreed in their Title II that all persons have the right to correspond by means of international telegraphs and that all states party agree to take all necessary measures to ensure the secrecy of correspondence and their good delivery.

In addition to general norms and agreement on definitions, such as what is a message, the treaty agreed on the tariffs to be charged in the national currencies of the states party. They also agreed that the treaty would be reviewed periodically to accommodate technological and economic developments.

In order to administer the agreements as well as to organize the review and amendment process the states decided to create an international organization, the International Telegraph Union. While this was a precursor of today's international organization, its secretariat was exclusively Swiss, who were considered by the other parties to be neutrals. The Swiss had also organized the International Committee of the Red Cross and had a precedent in providing secretariat services, including the Universal Postal Union (UPU). Both the ITU and the UPU were headquartered in Berne, Switzerland. Still, it reflected a functionalist model of international organization, where new organizations would be created because there was a need to preserve order when there was a change in technologies or other factors.[3]

An additional factor in the equation was that in some countries communication was a state-run enterprise, while in others, like the United States, the communication network was run by private corporations and, at the time, regulation was not considered a public responsibility. Even the United States decided to participate, at the Fourth Plenipotentiary Conference of the ITU in 1875. The ITU conferences provided an intergovernmental forum where both types of corporations could interact and agree.

As communications technology evolved, additional conventions were negotiated, to deal with telephony (as an amendment to the telegraphy convention), then radiocommunications, the latter culminating in the 1906 International Radiotelegraph Convention. As technology moved ahead the conventions were amended, or additional standards were adopted. In 1932, the Madrid Conference decided to merge the two basic conventions and rename the ITU as the International Telecommunications Union.

After the Second World War, like other previously existing international organizations, the ITU was reconstituted as a United Nations specialized agency. In addition to its plenary, the ITU set up, starting in the 1920s, consultative committees to coordinate technical studies, tests and measurements being carried out in the various fields of telecommunications, with a view to drawing up international standards. While many of the studies were done by private sector entities, whenever they had implications for global telecommunications, they became a responsibility of the ITU and its bodies. In 1956 the consultative committees were merged into a single Telephone and Telegraph Consultative Committee (CCITT). The ITU secretariat, since 1947 international rather than Swiss in character, organized the work and kept it going with its own research and analysis.

In addition to standards, the ITU also became involved in the allocation of frequency spectrums. Bandwidth for radio communications is a finite resource and to make sure that there were no competitors for the same frequencies, the ITU set up a procedure to allocate frequencies. Because the frequency spectrum is borderless, it has been considered a kind of global commons.

Similarly, when space satellites began to be launched for communication purposes, the ITU took the lead to allocate geo-stationary orbit slots, positions over the equator where satellites move at the same speed as the earth. Both spectrum allocation and orbit slots involved dividing up scarce goods among competing interests. Nevertheless, the ITU succeeded in doing so.

As long as telecommunications, considered "natural monopolies," were controlled either by government-owned enterprises or private enterprises with monopolistic rights, and the main channels were over landlines that passed over national borders much as telegraph lines in the nineteenth century, the ITU was able to maintain order through processes that were considered slow, but effective.[4] When technology and domestic politics in some of the larger industrial countries led to the breakup of the large telecoms and changes in standards had to be made quickly, the ITU began to experience problems.[5] When the Internet arrived full force in the mid-1990s, the ITU began to try to redefine its identity.

The content

Content of communication was regulated by three somewhat different regimes. One was the human rights regime that made guaranteeing freedom of expression an international obligation of states, where the United Nations Educational, Scientific and Cultural Organization (UNESCO) and the United Nations human rights program were especially concerned. The second was the regime for the protection of intellectual property, including that which could be sent over communication channels, managed by the World Intellectual Property Organization. The third was the World Trade Organization's (WTO) Agreement on Trade-Related Aspects of Intellectual Property Rights (TRIPS), negotiated in the 1986–94 Uruguay Round, which introduced intellectual property rules into the multilateral trading system

When the Universal Declaration on Human Rights was adopted in 1948, it included as one of its civil and political rights (Article 19):

> Everyone has the right to freedom of opinion and expression; this right includes freedom to hold opinions without interference and to seek, receive and impart information and ideas through any media and regardless of frontiers.

This was translated into international law by the International Covenant on Civil and Political Rights adopted by the United Nations in 1966 that entered into force in 1979. States party to that convention, numbering 160 by April 2007, have undertaken an obligation to ensure freedom of expression. However, Article 19,[6] while guaranteeing the right to freedom of expression including freedom to seek, receive and impart information and ideas of all kinds, regardless of frontiers, either orally, in writing or in print, in the form of art, or through any other media of his choice, provided for two exceptions. These are respect for the rights and reputations of others, and protection of national security, public order or public health or morals.

The second exception allowed states to tap telephone calls, intercept mail or censor newspapers, magazines or books. The first is more complex, because it depends on what "rights of others" means, but as international law has evolved, it has included intellectual property.

The Universal Declaration and its facilitative conventions are directed primarily at state behavior within a state's own borders. However, since they are international norms, all states are supposed to respect them and there is an "international interest" in how states comply. Over time, a compliance monitoring mechanism has evolved. In the case of the

Covenant on Civil and Political Rights, the Human Rights Committee reviews periodic reports from states party on their compliance with the convention. The committee's independent experts ask questions of the presenting governments and review replies in what is called the constructive dialogue. The committee has prepared a series of general comments on the convention's articles as part of its work over the years, including one on Article 19 in 1983. The comment did not detect any general problems with state compliance with the article, but, of course the comment was written before the Internet.

The Covenant assumes that states can control their borders and that domestic law can ensure that compliance takes place. The same is true with intellectual property.

As analyzed by Christopher May in this series, "When knowledge becomes subject to ownership, IPRs [Intellectual Property Rights] express the legal benefits of ownership, most importantly: the ability to charge rent for use; to receive compensation for loss; and to gather payment for transfer."[7] Two elements of IPRs are relevant to communication: copyrights and trademarks. Copyrights refer to literary or artistic intellectual property, the ownership of the content of books, paintings, photographs, music and films. Trademarks distinguish the products of one company from another and can be made up of "one or more distinctive words, letters, numbers, drawings or pictures, emblems or other graphic representations."[8]

Intellectual property is protected under national laws, which initially differed according to the tradition of each country regarding property rights. Some countries took a very restrictive view of rights, while others were more generous. However, when intellectual property was traded, conflicts between national systems became evident. For example, in one country, the author of a book and his or her heirs would own the content in perpetuity, while in another country, copying of a foreign book was not considered an infringement of the author's rights. There were differences about what could be copied and how.

As a result, in the mid-nineteenth century, European countries, pressed by authors like Victor Hugo, worked to establish a multilateral agreement on copyrights. This was reflected in the Berne Convention for the Protection of Literary and Artistic Works (Paris, 1871). In its Article 2, the convention said: "The works mentioned in this article shall enjoy protection in all countries of the Union. This protection shall operate for the benefit of the author and his successors in title."

However, the protections provided would be determined by the laws of each state. In addition, "The protection of this Convention shall not apply to news of the day or to miscellaneous facts having the character of mere items of press information."

In order to administer the Berne Convention, as well as the companion Paris Convention for the Protection of Industrial Property (relating to patents), the states party decided, in 1893, to create what was called the Bureaux Internationaux Réunis pour la Protection de la Propriété Intellectuelle (BIRPPI) with headquarters in Berne, Switzerland. The main function of the organization was to assist in cross-registering patents and copyrights, compiling and publishing information on changes in state legislation and practice, assisting in modifications of the original conventions and in negotiating new ones to address technological changes.

In 1928, the states members of the BIRPPI, met in Rome to discuss the new broadcasting technologies. As May put it:[9]

> there were clear differences of opinion between states that wanted to reserve the private rights for authors as they already did for other technologies of distribution, and those countries like Australia and New Zealand that saw broadcasting as a public service that should be unencumbered by private rights, reflecting the emerging public service ethos of broadcasting in countries with vast distances between small communities. Once again, a compromise solution was concluded that, while setting the parameters of choice, allowed individual states to shape the measures that were appropriate for their societies.

This function continued when, in 1967, the Bureaux were converted into the World Intellectual Property Organization and switched from a Swiss to an international secretariat. The disputes about which types of intellectual property would be covered and by what national means continued but the regime, based on territoriality, functioned.

Most of the disputes on intellectual property were resolved nationally, especially in the United States. One of the major decisions had to do with the use of video recorders by individuals to tape programs being broadcast over television. In a 1984 landmark case in the United States, Sony Corp vs. Universal Studios (the Betamax case), a divided Supreme Court held 5–4 that owners of video recorders were not violating copyrights by copying programs to watch later.[10] The extent to which "fair use" of copyrighted material permits copying and sharing of music, films, radio and television programs or books was not completely clear, and depended on national legislation. The Berne Convention itself, in Article 10 (2), states:

> It shall be a matter for legislation in the countries of the Union, and for special agreements existing or to be concluded between

them, to permit the utilization, to the extent justified by the purpose, of literary or artistic works by way of illustration in publications, broadcasts or sound or visual recordings for teaching, provided such utilization is compatible with fair practice.

Each state party was allowed to determine what constituted fair practice.

The creation of the World Trade Organization (WTO) added new dimension to content regulation when it negotiated the Agreement on Trade-Related Aspects of Intellectual Property Rights (TRIPS) during the Uruguay Round that led to the formation of the WTO. The need to include intellectual property as part of trade agreement was because the Berne and Paris conventions did not have clear enforcement provisions and, as the WTO itself says,[11]

The extent of protection and enforcement of these rights varied widely around the world; and as intellectual property became more important in trade, these differences became a source of tension in international economic relations. New internationally-agreed trade rules for intellectual property rights were seen as a way to introduce more order and predictability, and for disputes to be settled more systematically.

While the reach of the TRIPS covered all intellectual property, and it took the Berne and Paris Conventions as starting points, its main focus was on tradeable goods. These were usually physical products like records, tapes, films, art, and books. Like all traded goods, it was within the power of states to stop illegal products (like counterfeit editions) at the frontier. The TRIPS allowed copyright holders access to national remedies, and this added teeth to the copyright protection system. Interestingly, TRIPS only included the concept of fair use with regard to trademarks, rather than copyright.

After the Internet: the RATS problem

As long as IP protection was provided by the physical borders of states that joined the various international agreements, the system was essentially stable. The development of an essentially borderless Internet changed this, and was a major factor in creating a need for Internet governance. The effect of the Internet can be illustrated by what I will call the RATS problem.

In 1975, I was stationed in Islamabad, Pakistan with the United Nations Development Programme. One recreational activity in which I participated was the Rawalpindi Amateur Theatrical Society (RATS). Although Pakistan was a party to the Berne Convention, its enforcement was not very active, and RATS could put on any play without paying rights. If RATS had been in any of the many countries (like neighboring Afghanistan) that were not parties to the copyright conventions at all, any play—including those currently on Broadway in New York or the West End in London—could be put on without paying for the rights.

Before the Internet, this was not a real problem. It is highly unlikely that anyone would travel from New York or London to Rawalpindi to see a play put on by RATS. If they did, pressure could be put by the United States or the U.K. government to have the Pakistan government close down the play. Of course, if RATS put on its pirated play in Afghanistan, there would be no real recourse, but it is even more unlikely that anything would be done.

The same could be said for such IP violations as making illegal copies of records or books. The market in Pakistan was simply too small to worry about the problem.

The Internet changed all of this. If RATS decided to raise money by recording its production and then making it available for downloading, the product would be available globally, and would compete with licit examples. RATS could perform any play and video-stream it to the world and could archive it for downloading. Anyone, anywhere with a computer and sufficient bandwidth could see the play. RATS could charge for the download and pocket the money and none of it would go to the authors of the play or its publishers. If, instead of Pakistan, RATS was located in a country that was not part of the intellectual property regime, no one could bring RATS to court.

Of course, it is unlikely that many downloaders would be interested in a RATS production of a Broadway play, but suppose instead that it was putting the most recent release of the Dixie Chicks on its server. The same could be true of anyone making music, or films, or software, available for downloading without paying the owners of the copyrights. The Internet made the concept of broadcasting, or communication of content, completely different.

In short, the old system for regulating both communication and its content, based on international organizations who helped states deal with issues of interoperability and intellectual property based on national jurisdiction, was not clearly applicable to the Internet, and clearly some new form of governance would be required that took into account both the nature of the Internet and its different stakeholders.

3 The non-state actors

Engineers, entrepreneurs, and netizens

In its initial years, non-state actors largely ran the Internet and in some aspects, they still do. Computer and other information technology professionals deal with engineering standards, private sector and academic professionals deal with application standards, private corporations provide investment resources and the individual users of the Internet have their rights defended by civil society organizations. Each of these actors has developed an approach to governance in their areas and this has helped define the broader approach to Internet governance.

The initial dominance and subsequent role of non-state actors derived from the Internet's origin as a project to link scientists in the United States. In the 1960s and 1970s, a major source of research funding for universities was the United States Department of Defense, which underwrote scientific research that might have defense implications through its Defense Advanced Projects Administration (DARPA).

As described by the Internet Society's *Brief History of the Internet*,[1] computer scientists had become interested in networking computers over long telephone lines, but had found that they needed packet switching (see Chapter 1) to make that happen. DARPA funded a number of scientists led by Vinton Cerf and Robert Kahn to develop what was called ARPANET. This included developing the switching specifications, but also the Transmission Control Protocol/Internet Protocol (TCP/IP), software that allowed data to pass from one computer to another over communications lines.

While the funds came from government sources, colleagues who were mostly academic administered the funds. These academics were more concerned with openness and innovation than with rules. Coordination of developments in networking, including software and hardware, was perceived to be necessary and DARPA in 1983 established what came to be called the Internet Architecture Board (IAB). This included, as a self-standing entity, the Internet Engineering Task

Force (IETF). The IAB was initially made up of a mixture of government officials, academic researchers and computer professionals from the private sector. By 1992, DARPA had ended its interest in the Internet and United States Government concern was vested in the National Science Foundation. However, the government interest had become secondary to commercial and academic interests, and the sponsorship of the IAB was moved to the Internet Society, a non-governmental organization. The Internet Society describes itself as

> a professional membership society with more than 100 organization and over 20,000 individual members in over 180 countries. It provides leadership in addressing issues that confront the future of the Internet, and is the organization home for the groups responsible for Internet infrastructure standards, including the Internet Engineering Task Force (IETF) and the Internet Architecture Board (IAB).
>
> Thailand Chapter of the Internet Society, http://www.isoc-th.org/

The dominant organizational method of these non-state actors, as will be seen, is the horizontal network, rather than the vertical networks that characterize governments and inter-governmental organizations. Technological change is so rapid that formal structures do not react swiftly enough and, as a result, these non-state actors became the principal players in the management of the Internet.

Technical standards: the engineers

The technical heart of the Internet is a series of standards that, once adopted, allow the Internet to function seamlessly. The main body to determine these standards is the Internet Engineering Task Force (IETF) run under the auspices of the Internet Society. The IETF operates through working groups to deal with specific technical issues. In July 2007, there were 120 working groups in eight areas. The areas included a general area on intellectual property rights and specific areas on Applications (9), Internet (29), Operations and Management (17), Real-time Applications and Infrastructure (17), Routing (15), Security (17), and Transport (15).

Technical standards problems are suggested by members and, if there is enough interest, a working group is formed, with a defined terms of reference. An example is the working group on the internationalization of e-mail addresses. As the working group's site says:

> Since early in the effort to internationalize domain names, which resulted in the standards associated with IDNA, it has been

understood that internationalization of email address local parts is required. At the same time, email address internationalization poses a series of special problems. Constraints on the interpretation of local-parts by any system other than the final delivery one make address encoding nearly impossible. The need to use addresses in both the email envelope and in header fields, and to do so in ways that are at least compatible, suggests that this is not a simple and isolated problem. This working group will address one basic approach to email internationalization.

> Internet Engineering Task Force, Working Group
> on Email Address Internationalization,
> http://www.ietf.org/html.charters/eai-charter.html

The approach being studied has to do with how address headers in packets could be modified.

Each working group has a chair, either elected or self-designated. In this case, there are two chairs, an engineer from Norway who works for Cisco Systems, and an engineer from China who works for the China Internet Network Information Center. The process is roughly the same for each working group and has been established since the beginning of the IETF.

The process of agreeing on standards is laborious, but has been organized since 1996.[2] The IETF defines the Internet as "a loosely-organized international collaboration of autonomous, interconnected networks, supports host-to-host communication through voluntary adherence to open protocols and procedures defined by Internet Standards." An Internet Standard is further defined as "a specification that is stable and well-understood, is technically competent, has multiple, independent, and interoperable implementations with substantial operational experience, enjoys significant public support, and is recognizably useful in some or all parts of the Internet."

The approach has two key dimensions. The standard has to work, and the technical people who work on the Internet have to agree that it is useful enough that everyone will accept and use it. Because of the interconnectedness of networks, any change in the standard governing one aspect could affect other aspects. As a result the IETF procedure is designed to ensure that any standard agreed has been sufficiently tested and will not affect the stability of the Internet as a whole.

To ensure this, each possible standard is run though a sequence of stages. Anyone can propose a possible standard by posting it as a draft. If there is enough interest in it, the Internet Engineering Steering Group, made up of the IETF chair and the area directors as well as several liaison officers, will designate it a "proposed standard." As defined, this means that it "is generally stable, has resolved known design choices, is believed to be well-understood, has received significant community review, and appears to enjoy enough community interest to be considered valuable." After some six months in this status, with further review, usually in the context of a working group, and further demonstration of an ability to work in different networks and languages it can become a "draft standard." After at least another four months, or the next IETF meeting (whichever is later), and a positive recommendation by a working group, the IESG can propose to issue it as a standard with a two-week Last Call for final objections. Once given the status of an Internet Standard, it can be used throughout the Internet.

The central coordinating body of the IETF is the Steering Group. It can determine which proposals go through the next steps, engages in mediation of disputes and generally ensures order in the IETF. If the IETF were an intergovernmental body, this would be the function provided by a bureau, consisting of the elected officers. In the IETF, the elections are held annually. The procedure for the elections is different from most public organizations. There are certain rules. Half of the IESG positions are up for election every year, with incumbents potentially renewable. Each year a nominations committee (NomCom) is established. This is done by requesting volunteers from among the IETF members, who self-select. From these volunteers, the committee is selected by random procedures. This guarantees that the nominating committee is not biased, reflects the distribution of volunteers and is therefore credible.

The NomCom considers candidates for the position and then selects, on the basis of consensus, the agreed candidates. These are usually then confirmed at the next meeting of the IETF. The process, while long (about seven months), is smooth, because the composition of the NomCom is credible to the membership.

The IETF process is called "rough consensus" and the Task Force was a pioneer in this. Consensus as a concept does not have a formal definition. The IETF says:[3]

> Working groups make decisions through a "rough consensus" process. IETF consensus does not require that all participants agree although this is, of course, preferred. In general, the dominant view of the working group shall prevail. ... Consensus can be determined by a show of hands, humming, or any other means on which the WG agrees (by rough consensus, of course). Note that 51% of the working group does not qualify as "rough consensus" and 99% is better than rough. It is up to the Chair to determine if rough consensus has been reached.

This is similar to the consensus process used at the intergovernmental level (except for the humming) and involves the same art by a chair. In the consensus system practiced by the IETF, a single objector would not stop the consensus, but if there were several objections, the chair might have to decide that consensus had not be achieved. In the inter-governmental process, where states are formally equal, a single objec-tor could halt consensus, although in practice it would depend on which state. (If it is the United States, it would carry weight, but if it were Palau, Andorra or San Marino, perhaps not.)

Given the importance of the process followed by the IETF, its com-position is important. The IETF is defined as "a large open international community of network designers, operators, vendors, and researchers concerned with the evolution of the Internet architecture and the smooth operation of the Internet. It is open to any interested indivi-dual."[4] IETF decision-making processes mean that members need to be active if their views are to be heard. In that sense, operational membership is self-defined. So, who are these operational members?

This can be seen in the listed chairs of all of the 120 working groups functioning in September 2007. There was a total of 242 individuals. Table 3.1 shows the distribution of chairs according to several criteria.

By far the largest number of members, as well as chairs, came from the private sector, especially computer companies like Cisco Systems that draw their business from the Internet. Most are middle-level tech-nicians rather than senior management. If they were civil servants (almost none of whom are represented), they would be what is called middle management.

Table 3.1 Chairs in the IETF, September 2007

Total	*Number*	*%*
By region in which member works		
United States	173	71
Other OECD	56	23
Developing country	13	6
By stakeholder group		
Government	9	4
Private sector	189	78
Computer company	100	41
Telecommunications	75	31
Other	14	6
NGO	14	6
Academic	26	11

There were some differences between members who were resident in the United States compared with those who were non-U.S. (all from developed countries) as can be seen in Table 3.2. They were somewhat more likely not to be from the private sector and, for those in the private sector, somewhat more likely to be from telecommunications rather than computer companies. This probably reflects the reality of global industries where computer companies are more likely to be U.S.-based, whereas telecommunications companies are more evenly distributed.

The IETF is not the only engineering standard setter, although it is the main one for the Internet. The International Electro-technical Commission, located in Geneva, Switzerland "prepares and publishes international standards for all electrical, electronic and related technologies. These serve as a basis for national standardization and as references when drafting international tenders and contracts."[5] Similarly, the Institute of Electrical and Electronics Engineers, Inc. (IEEE) sets key standards for wireless communication (IEEE 802). These function in a similar way to the IETF.

Technical standards: the designers

The IETF is concerned with the Internet architecture, but does not deal with the basic applications of the Net. This has been the province of the World Wide Web Consortium (W3C), a formal organization of designers who set standards for the Web.

The Internet only became popular when it became useful for exchanging information. One of the early methods was to link information by what was called hyperlinks. Tim Berners-Lee, then working at the European Organization for Nuclear Research (CERN), wanted to find a way to organize the vast amounts of information being produced. He started from a variant of what was called "hypertext," or "human readable information linked together in an unconstrained way." Berners-Lee's

Table 3.2 Type of organization for IETF members by country of residence

Country of residence		*U.S.A.*	*OECD/ non-U.S.A.*	*Total*
Organization	Non-private	17%	29%	19%
	Computer	50%	26%	31%
	Telecom	28%	38%	27%
	Others	5%	7%	5%
Total		173	69	242

design included the idea that information could be stored on a computer functioning as a server and could be accessed by software called a browser. He concluded:[6]

> We should work toward a universal linked information system, in which generality and portability are more important than fancy graphics techniques and complex extra facilities.
>
> The aim would be to allow a place to be found for any information or reference which one felt was important, and a way of finding it afterwards. The result should be sufficiently attractive to use that the information contained would grow past a critical threshold, so that the usefulness the scheme would in turn encourage its increased use.

The result of the effort was the World Wide Web, including a server, a client program consisting of a browser and editor and the "HyperText Markup Language" (HTML), which is the language for formatting documents with the capability for hypertext links that became the primary publishing format for the Web. Combined with the Internet packet switching protocol, this produced the information revolution that now constitutes the Internet. Subsequent developments have increased the capacity of individuals to access the Internet and have incorporated the media, graphics and search engines that characterize the Internet in 2008.

To provide order in the improvement of standards for the World Wide Web, which quickly became the main vehicle for published Internet content (and, eventually, even for e-mails), Berners-Lee founded the World Wide Web Consortium (W3C) in 1994. Its mission is "To lead the World Wide Web to its full potential by developing protocols and guidelines that ensure long-term growth for the Web."[7]

Housed at the Massachusetts Institute of Technology (MIT) Laboratory for Computer Science, where Berners-Lee moved from CERN, the W3C was supported by both DARPA and the European Commission, making it an international NGO. Unlike the IETF, where members are individuals, the W3C members are organizations, primarily from the private sector. W3C describes itself as "industry consortium dedicated to building consensus around Web technologies."[8] Table 3.3 shows the membership as of September 2007.

Like the IETF, the majority of the members are from private sector corporations, although the participation by stakeholders is more diverse. Within the private sector, the dominant source of members is computer companies rather than the balance between computer and

Table 3.3 Membership in the W3C, September 2007

	Number	%
Total	443	100
By region in which member works		
United States	182	41
Other OECD	183	41
Developing country	77	18
Stakeholder group		
Government	40	9
Private sector	286	65
Computer company	206	47
Telecommunications	40	9
Other	43	10
NGO	62	14
Academic	54	12

Table 3.4 Country of W3C member residency by type of organization

Type of organization	Country			Total
	Developing	Developed	USA	
Academia	20%	17%	4%	12%
Government	20%	11%	4%	9%
NGO	12%	14%	16%	15%
Private corporation	49%	58%	76%	65%
Total	41	219	183	443

telecommunications companies that is found in the IETF. There are also more NGOs and academics working in the W3C. Unlike the IETF, the members are more geographically balanced, although heavily weighted to developed countries.

There are differences, however, by the country of residence. The members from the United States are overwhelmingly from private corporations, while the half of non-U.S. members not working for private corporations are relatively evenly divided between academics, government officials and members of non-governmental organizations (Table 3.4).

The W3C is like IETF in that it operates through working groups, whose members are volunteers, goes through a sequence of stages before agreeing on a W3C Recommendation, the equivalent of the IETF Internet Standard. Like the IETF, the W3C agrees on recommendations by consensus.

Unlike the IETF, the W3C has a formal decision-making structure. Each member organization designates a representative to the Advisory Committee. This committee elects the members of two standing bodies, the Technical Architecture Group (TAG), to help resolve Consortium-wide technical issues; and the Advisory Board (AB), to help resolve Consortium-wide non-technical issues, and to manage the evolution of the W3C process.[9]

While the process appears to be cumbersome, the W3C has achieved major agreements on web protocols that are reported on their web site[10] (see Figure 3.1).

Commercial application standards: the entrepreneurs

The Internet runs on computers, uses telecommunications services and has many content providers, all of which—with the exception of government-run telephone companies—are in the private sector. Unlike the open standard-setters represented by the IETF and W3C, which exist because of a common interest on the part of all stakeholders to have agreed standards for the Internet, private computer corporations make their money by having proprietary applications for which consumers pay. Telecommunications companies make their money by renting out physical lines and providing switching and other services. While they are dependent on the underlying protocols, they have an incentive to keep their own software closed. Some of the largest makers of computers, their operating systems and their components, have fought to protect their intellectual property. Some, like Microsoft in operating systems, Apple in downloadable music, Intel in computer chips and Qualcomm in mobile phone technology, have achieved near-monopolies in their field.

While proprietary standards for specific products have been common in the private sector for centuries, the Internet has made them more controversial, since they can affect how well the Internet functions. As a result, private corporations have joined not-for-profit standard-setting bodies as a means of ensuring that their proprietary software is compatible and interoperable. However, when one corporation becomes dominant, governments have been induced to regulate them.

The most dramatic case is Microsoft, whose operating system is dominant in personal computers. In order to take advantage of the Internet, Microsoft bundled its browser, Internet Explorer, in its operating system to the exclusion of other browsers. This had the effect of driving its main competitor, Netscape—a browser developed at the University of Illinois—almost out of business. Other companies complained and the United States government sued Microsoft. In the case, *United States*

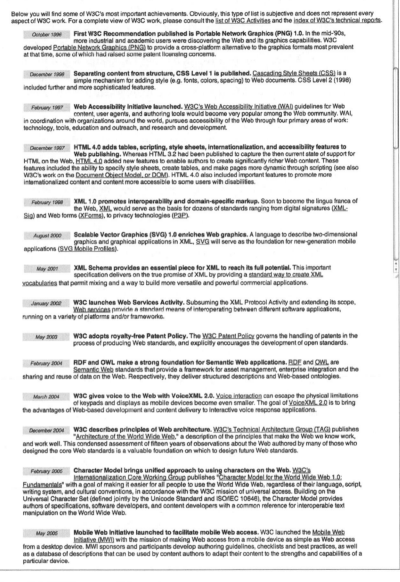

Figure 3.1 W3C accomplishments.

vs. Microsoft, a federal judge ruled against Microsoft. The judge, Thomas Penfield Jackson, concluded:[11]

> To the detriment of consumers, however, Microsoft has done much more than develop innovative browsing software of commendable quality and offer it bundled with Windows at no additional charge. As has been shown, Microsoft also engaged in a concerted series of actions designed to protect the applications barrier to entry, and hence its monopoly power, from a variety of middleware threats, including Netscape's web browser and Sun's implementation of Java. Many of these actions have harmed consumers in ways that are immediate and easily discernible. They have also caused less direct, but nevertheless serious and far-reaching, consumer harm by distorting competition.

As part of the settlement, Microsoft agreed to open up aspects of its operating system to third-party browser (and other applications) makers.

The issue was not resolved, however, until 2007, when the European Court of First Instance—an appeals court—affirmed a 2004 ruling that Microsoft had violated European competition rules by making it impossible for third-party Internet media viewers to run on Microsoft's Windows operating system. In the suit, Microsoft was supported by a number of other private corporations, while the European Commission was supported by several associations advocating open or free software.[12] The judgment is expected to affect other dominant players who use proprietary software to ensure market dominance, including Apple, Intel and Qualcomm.[13] A broader implication is that these corporations will increasingly have to participate in Internet governance.

As noted in Chapter 2, telecommunications corporations were major participants in the work of the ITU, and the arrangements provided order in their businesses. Most telecommunications corporations were either government-owned or publicly-regulated monopolies who could agree on transnational standards among themselves. With the deregulation of telecommunications in the United States and the privatization of telecommunications in many countries in Europe, the system became less functional.

The growth of the Internet had several additional consequences for the telecommunications companies. First, an increasing part of their business consisted of providing "last-mile" access to the Internet, connections of individuals to Internet service providers (ISPs) over telephone lines. However, here they faced competition from other access providers, including cable companies, satellite providers and even electricity companies, all of whom could also transmit Internet packets, sometimes faster than the telecommunications companies could. Second, the alternative access providers, thanks to the Voice Over Internet protocols (voip) that had been developed when the Internet was Arpanet, could provide inexpensive telecommunications in competition with telecoms. In some cases, like Skype, the "Global P2P Telephony Company," a company registered in Luxembourg and using person-to-person (P2P), Internet telephony is free, with company profits based on advertising and connecting to mobile or land-line phones.

Telecommunications companies also have had to become interested in Internet governance to help regulate a technologically mobile international environment. This is related to problems of national regulation of networks that was based on the older principles, as has been documented by Russell Neuman, Lee McKnight, and Richard Jay Solomon.[14]

The third group of corporations concerned with the Internet includes content providers. These are companies who provide text, videos, music and search engines, among other things, that are distributed by packet switching and use various Internet and web protocols. Their interest is to ensure that content is protected, but can use existing systems. Much of their concern is with intellectual property, as we will see in Chapter 4. They are also concerned with protocol that will facilitate content delivery. Often, as in the case of Apple with its iTunes service that provides downloadable music and video feeds (television programs or entire movies), they are also hardware and software makers. They also include telecommunications companies, particularly those using wireless methods that can connect, through browsers, with the Internet and also download content.

Freedom of use: the netizens

The non-state actors noted so far, with the exception of the IETF, are largely organizations, particularly from the private sector, concerned with technical specifications, and through them, policy. There is an equally large group of non-state actors concerned with the openness and freedom of the Internet. They have been termed "netizens," a term coined by Michael Hauben in 1995 as a contraction of net and citizen. In his book, *Netizens: On the History and Impact of Usenet and the Internet*, he defines netizens as[15]

> people who care about Usenet and the bigger Net and work towards building the cooperative and collective nature which benefits the larger world. These are people who work towards developing the

Net. In this second case, Netizen represents positive activity, and no adjective need be used. Both uses have spread from the online community, appearing in newspapers, magazines, television, books and other off-line media. As more and more people join the online community and contribute towards the nurturing of the Net and towards the development of a great shared social wealth, the ideas and values of Netizenship spread.

The Usenet, to which he refers, is a network run by volunteers with common interests. As Wikipedia describes it, Usenet

> is a global, decentralized, distributed Internet discussion system that evolved from a general purpose UUCP architecture of the same name. It was conceived by Duke University graduate students Tom Truscott and Jim Ellis in 1979. Users read and post e-mail-like messages (called "articles" or "posts") to one or more of a number of categories, called newsgroups. Usenet resembles bulletin board systems (BBS) in most respects, and is the precursor to the various Internet forums which are widely used today.[16]

The original Usenet groups did not have a central server. Instead, a system of servers, usually on individual computers, served to hold the network together. These evolved into Internet forums, most of which are web-based.

The Usenet idea was that the Internet could link persons with similar interests regardless of their geographic location. It would permit the free flow of information necessary for democracy. The netizens' concern was to protect the openness of the channel at all costs. As Hauben stated, in the last chapter of his book,[17]

> This is an exciting time to see the democratic ideas of some great political thinkers beginning to be practical. James Mill wrote that for government to serve the people, it must be watched over by the people utilizing an uncensored press. Freedom of the press also makes possible the debate necessary for people to form well founded opinions. Usenet and e.g., Cleveland Free-Net [an experiment in a publicly available network] are contemporary examples of the uncensored accessible press required by Mill. These networks are also the result of hard work by many people aspiring for more democracy. However, to keep these forms developing and spreading requires constant work from those dedicated to the hard fight for democracy.

Newsgroups, as these Usenet groups are called are varied, changeable and chaotic. On my news server (Giganet) on 18 September 2007, there were 107,127 distinct groups on which individuals were posting. The posts included messages, pictures, sound files and video files. The persons running the groups were largely anonymous.

The Netizens as defenders of the right to communicate could trace at least some of their origins to hackers in the United States. This was well before the Internet as we know it developed, in 1990, when the main element of the Internet was the bulletin board, a space on which different persons could place and share documents.[18] Throughout the 1980s individuals had tried to obtain free long-distance telephone calls by various devices (including whistling the correct tones to dial). Some computer programmers, who found breaking into corporate communications systems exciting, found telephone switching centers exciting targets. However, on 15 January 1990, there was a major crash of the AT&T long-distance switching system. While this was probably caused by a malfunction within the system, one presumed culprit was hackers who, the telephone companies believed, could cause the system to crash by their intrusions into the computer systems. The telephone companies convinced law enforcement authorities to apply laws passed in the 1980s to control crime (such as the 1986 Computer Fraud and Abuse Act).

In 1989 a hacker in Georgia penetrated a computer of the BellSouth telephone company and copied an internal technical document. He then loaded it on a bulletin board in Chicago and eventually an edited version of the document was published in an electronic newsletter. Pushed by telephone companies who were afraid of computer fraud, law enforcement agencies in Georgia, Illinois and Texas (as well as others) collaborated in an effort to apprehend the hackers. If all they had done was to go after those hackers who were clearly committing fraud, there would probably have been no problem. However, the law enforcement agencies went after the owners of servers on which some of the documents had been stored, even though the owners had no knowledge of this.

These actions appeared to some Internet pioneers to threaten the freedom of communication over the Internet. Two of them, John Perry Barlow and Mitch Kapor, founded what they called the Electronic Frontier Foundation (EFF), to fight what they perceived were efforts to control the new medium. Barlow was a songwriter for the rock band the Grateful Dead, and a pioneer in computer journalism. Mitch Kapor was the the co-inventor of the spreadsheet program Lotus 1-2-3 and the founder of Lotus Development Corporation, representing in that way the new entrepreneurs that would later drive the "dot.com" revolution of the late 1990s. Barlow wrote an essay entitled "Crime and Puzzlement," in which he characterized the Internet in this way:[19]

> Cyberspace, in its present condition, has a lot in common with the 19th Century West. It is vast, unmapped, culturally and legally ambiguous, verbally terse (unless you happen to be a court stenographer), hard to get around in, and up for grabs. Large institutions already claim to own the place, but most of the actual natives are solitary and independent, sometimes to the point of sociopathy. It is, of course, a perfect breeding ground for both outlaws and new ideas about liberty.

After reviewing how law enforcement was dealing with cybercrime, which he believed was excessive in terms of the crimes involved, Barlow announced:

> But as of today (in early June of 1990), Mitch and I are legally constituting the Computer Liberty Foundation, a two (or possibly three) man organization which will raise and disburse funds for education, lobbying, and litigation in the areas relating to digital speech and the extension of the Constitution into Cyberspace.
> ...
> The Computer Liberty Foundation will fund, conduct, and support legal efforts to demonstrate that the Secret Service has exercised prior restraint on publications, limited free speech, conducted improper seizure of equipment and data, used undue force, and generally conducted itself in a fashion which is arbitrary, oppressive, and unconstitutional.

The Foundation was eventually called the Electronic Frontier Foundation, which started by filing a suit on behalf of one of those whose computer had been seized by the United States Secret Service. Eventually the Foundation won and subsequently became a recognized voice of Internet users' civil rights.[20] It attracted both computer professionals and lawyers specializing in civil rights. In 2007 its board of directors includes, in addition to John Perry Barlow, five technology entrepreneurs who made their fortunes during the dot.com period, two professors of computer sciences and two professors of law who specialize in the Internet, including Lawrence Lessig, of whom more later.

In John Perry Barlow's manifesto, he expressed an intention to cooperate with another group, the Computer Professionals for Social

Responsibility (CPSR), which had been formed in the 1980s originally to express concern about the increasing use of computing technology in military applications. It was a United States based non-governmental organization that, in 1991 began to sponsor annual conferences on Computers, Freedom and Privacy.[21] The CPSR was initially concerned about policies of the United States government but gradually has extended its interests internationally and in 2004 was given formal accreditation as a non-governmental organization in consultative status with the United Nations Economic and Social Council, the highest international formal recognition of NGOs.

In 2007, the 10-member board of directors of the CPSR included nationals of the United States, Canada, the United Kingdom, Ghana and Japan.

While organizations like the Electronic Frontier Foundation and the CPSR were focusing on rights, another organization was trying to use the Internet for development. One of the early growth areas in the Internet were Usenet-based networks of individuals sharing a common interest. Individual networks working in the area of the environment were among the first to organize themselves into a global association. In 1990, the Association for Progressive Communication (APC) was founded by networks including the Institute for Global Communication (IGC from the United States), GreenNet (U.K.), NordNet (Sweden), Web Networks (Canada), Alternex/IBASE (Brazil), Nicarao/CRIES (Nicaragua), and Pegasus (Australia).[22] The mission of the organization (formally adopted in 1997) was to be "a global network of civil society organisations whose mission is to empower and support organisations, social movements and individuals in and through the use of information and communication technologies to build strategic communities and initiatives for the purpose of making meaningful contributions to equitable human development, social justice, participatory political processes and environmental sustainability."[23]

In the pre-Internet period, APC communicated by e-mail and computer connections, but was the largest of the networks linking civil society groups and, in the preparations for the 1992 United Nations Conference on Environment and Development (UNCED) (the Earth Summit), the UN secretariat called on APC to provide electronic information about the conference as well as to permit civil society groups to lobby. At the conference itself, APC provided an online conference facility for delegates and NGOs, a practice that they continued at the United Nations Conference on Human Rights in Vienna in 1993 and, most visibly, at the Fourth United Nations Conference on Women in Beijing in 1995.

Recognized internationally as a voice for persons using ICT, especially in developing countries, APC has become a visible stakeholder in the Internet.

Non-state actors were the major players in the origins of the Internet and in its early governance. They did so using procedures that were more open than those of governments, but also like those used by governments through consensus decision-making. They established their importance for both technical matters and for guarding the openness of communication. Both were tested when the domain name problem emerged to challenge the non-state status quo, as we shall now see.

4 Solving the domain name problem
Internet governance is born

Milton Mueller began his classic study *Ruling the Root*[1] with this picture:

> For two days in July 1998, one hundred and fifty people gathered
> in a windowless hotel convention room in Reston, Virginia. The
> crowd comprised techies in T-shirts, trademark lawyers in suits,
> academic and business people, and a small but significant number
> of Europeans, Latin Americans, and Asians. The meeting had an
> ambitious goal: to "prepare a model, a set of common principles, a
> structure and general charter provisions" for the formation of a
> global governance body for an Internet naming and addressing
> authority.

The comfortable world of the technical people who considered the
Internet their province was challenged by the consequences of growth,
which had both economic and regulatory dimensions, and the United
States government took steps to define a new approach to governance,
with long-term consequences that are still felt today.

Governance of the Internet had become a policy and institutional
issue only in 1998, when the United States government decided that it had
to establish an institutional basis for maintaining order in the core functions of the growing communication medium. The trigger was a problem
with intellectual property combined with issues of domestic monopoly
power and fears of incursion by the international public sector. The result
was the creation of what is now a central, and controversial, institution,
the Internet Corporation for Assigned Names and Numbers (ICANN).

The story about how ICANN was created tells us a great deal about
the difficulties in achieving agreed governance of the Internet and provides
a point of departure for looking at the institutional frontier that is emerging ten years later. It explains why Internet governance, as Mueller
described it, involved geeks, governments and corporations, and still does.

Scarcity and monopoly—Network Solutions under attack

As noted in Chapter 1, the critical element of the Internet is its addressing system. Each sender and receiver has to have a unique address or e-mails (and web sites) will not get to them. The initial addresses were numbers, but these soon became cumbersome and the persons using the Internet sought an easier form of identification. They hit upon the idea of domain names. Domain names were intended to describe the kinds of persons or institutions that were associated with a given set of numbers. After some discussion in the Internet Architecture Board, the participants decided that there should be five top-level domains, for specific groups. Table 4.1 shows the result, as of 1998, including who should control allocation of names.

In 1998, there was only one registrar for the five common domain names.[2] Network Solutions, Inc. was a subsidiary of a large defense contractor, Science Applications International Corporation (SAIC). Charles Kuhlman and I described how they became the registrar in our 1998 paper that analyzed the controversy.[3]

The assignment of names to domains in preference to numbers was a convenience for the early users of the Internet. The responsibility for assigning numbers was delegated by the United States government to an independent entity called the International Assigned Numbers Authority, headed by Professor Jon Postel of the University of Southern California. The IANA was primarily concerned with ensuring that duplicate numbers were not assigned and that assigned numbers were entered into a central directory (the root directory). IANA assigned the country codes for domain names, including that for the United States (.us).

The attachment of names to the numbers which were not country-specific, the generic top-level domain names (gTLDs) for .com, .org and .edu was the responsibility of another entity, which was working

Table 4.1 Original top-level domain names

Domain name	Group	Registrar
com	Business and individuals	Network Solutions Incorporated
org	Not-for-profit organizations	Network Solutions Incorporated
net	Networks	Network Solutions Incorporated
edu	Universities	Network Solutions Incorporated
gov	United States Government (other than armed forces)	Network Solutions Incorporated
mil	United States Armed Forces	United States Department of Defense

under a subcontract from the National Science Foundation, as a result of competitive bidding. The entity was a private company, Network Solutions, Inc. (NSI), functioning as InterNic. It is a commentary on the size of the Internet when the contract was issued and NSI began to register domain names, that the NSF provided a subvention to NSI to cover the costs of what was in effect a free service.

As the Internet increased in size, the number of registrations increased dramatically. NSI made a decision to charge for site registration, a decision that was extremely unpopular among those persons who believed that the Internet should be, in effect, a free good. The cost factor, plus some management problems in NSI caused by the sudden increase in volume, caused many netizens to see NSI as a potential monopoly. NSI's policy of registering any name that was not duplicative also produced problems when other persons appropriated trademarked names. A number of entrepreneurs, sensing the potential growth of the Internet, registered blocks of names and, in some cases, resold them to the trademark holders in what was perceived as a form of extortion. Court cases based on trademark infringement began to emerge. As the number of domains registered under .com increased into the millions, a shortage of good names was perceived.

By 1997, registering domain names for a fee had become a major cash cow for Network Solutions Incorporated (NSI). It also got into significant problems with intellectual property since it registered domain names that were trademarked by other companies. Many of these then sued NSI but the company's profits were enormous. As the judgment in one of the many court cases about trademark violation put it:[4]

> Under a contract with the National Science Foundation, NSI manages domain name registrations for the ".com," ".net," ".org," ".edu," and ".gov" top-level domains. The contract authorizes NSI to charge $100 for an initial two-year registration and $50 annually starting the third year. NSI registers approximately 100,000 Internet domain names per month. (Graves Decl. ¶5.) Registration applications are made via e-mail and in more than 90% of registrations no human intervention takes place. (Graves Depo. at 54.) On average, a new registration occurs approximately once every 20 seconds.
>
> (*Id.* at 47–48)

NSI screened domain name applications against its registry to prevent repeated registrations of the same name. It also maintained a directory linking domain names with the IP numbers of domain name servers that were then entered into the IANA root directory.

Among major constituency groups like the Internet Society, some of the major telecommunications companies and a growing group of Internet service providers (ISPs), the problems with domain registration affected both the order and the procedures of the Internet. The NSF subcontract with Network Solutions was due to expire in 1998, and they decided to develop an alternative. In the tradition of informal governance, they formed what was called the International Ad-Hoc Committee (IAHC) to develop an alternative method of domain registry.

The resulting proposal, evolved under the "rough consensus" model that had traditionally governed Internet standards, included the creation of seven new top-level domains, the establishment of a large number of registrars, the creation of a central registry of names and numbers, the creation of a dispute resolution machinery and the establishment of an Internet policy institution. Significantly, it included the involvement of two international organizations, the ITU to register the registrars and the WIPO to manage the dispute resolution mechanism.

The proposal, called the Memorandum of Understanding on Top-Level Domains, set in motion the process leading to the current institutional structure of Internet governance, with a shift to both multilateral and multi-stakeholder institutions.

The MoU-tld controversy

The Memorandum of Understanding (MoU) was signed by 215 parties at ITU headquarters in May 1997. Memoranda of Understanding were a common method within the ITU for establishing standards without a formal intergovernmental agreement, although their legitimacy was enforced by their status within the international telecommunications regime. Table 4.2 shows the breakdown by region of the signers, and 70 percent came from outside the United States, mostly from Western Europe.[5]

The MoU created a mechanism that included a Policy Advisory Board, made up of representatives of the various Internet constituencies, a Policy Oversight Committee (POC) made up of elected representatives of constituency groups and a Council of Registrars (CORE), composed of those entities who were selected to register domain names, to oversee the domain name registration process.

The net effect of the MoU would be to internationalize Internet governance, at least in terms of one of its central functions.

Table 4.2 Geographical distribution of original signers of the gTLD-MoU

Region	Number	%
Asia	41	19.1
Eastern Europe	6	2.8
Western Europe	84	39.1
Africa	4	1.9
Latin America and Caribbean	8	3.7
Canada	9	4.2
U.S.A.	63	29.3
Total	215	100.0

Source: Calculated by Mathiason and Kuhlman from ITU, List of Signatories of the Generic Top-Level Domain Memorandum of Understanding (gTLD-MoU), 1997.

While for the "Internet establishment," the MoU solved what was becoming a major problem, for others, including NSI, it constituted both a threat and an affront. A number felt that it gave too much power to international organizations. Others felt that it bypassed national regulatory mechanisms, especially in the United States. Still others felt than any regulation whatsoever threatened the open character of the Internet. Pressure was put on governments, especially that of the United States, not to accept the MoU.

The United States government acts

The United States government was put under particular pressure. As the government which had funded much, but not all, of the development of the Internet and which, through IANA and the NSI contract, maintained the root directory, it felt a particular responsibility. At the same time, the United States federal government was in a stage of trying to deregulate industries. Cross-pressured, the U.S. delegation to the ITU did not sign the MoU and sent conflicting signals about where it stood.

Clearly unsure of its position, the United States government reverted to procedures that were used nationally when regulations were contemplated, a period of public comment. The national entity concerned with telecommunications regulation, the National Telecommunications and Information Administration (NTIA) issued a request for comments on 16 June 1997 based on a series of specific questions about Internet governance in general and about detailed aspects of the domain name registration question.

Some 282 distinct comments were received over the comment period in July and August 1997. Based on these, an advisor to the U.S. president, Ira Magaziner, began to prepare a proposal for management of the Internet. Magaziner was a long-time friend of President Bill Clinton who had been a coordinator of a controversial and ill-fated effort to reform health care in the United States (under the direction of Hillary Rodham Clinton, then First Lady). He had worked as a consultant in the telecommunications and computer industries and was appointed by President Clinton to be the administration's Internet czar.

The Green Paper

The proposal was finally issued in what was called a "Green Paper," a draft policy statement. The Green Paper sought to resolve the dilemma by creating a new structure for domain name assignment through the devolution of the IANA function to a non-profit public corporation located in the United States, creating five new generic top-level domain names, undertaking a study of Internet governance and, as a transitional matter, extending the Network Solutions registration contract until the details of the new system were worked out.

The Green Paper was submitted for public comment on 20 February 1998. By the end of March 1998, over 500 distinct comments had been received. They ranged from short comments favoring one or another model through detailed, well elaborated comments on specific issues raised in the Green Paper as well as on the Green Paper itself. They included comments from individuals and from the European Union.

The purpose of public comments in the United States is to gauge whether there is a consensus about a proposed policy and if one does not exist, what the different positions are. Who makes the comments in this case tells a great deal about the interest groups at the beginning of Internet governance. Table 4.3, drawn from Kuhlman's and my analysis of the comments made in 1997 and 1998 on the U.S. proposal, shows the variety of interested parties.[6]

The distribution by type of commenters was about the same between the 1997 comment period and the comments on the Green Paper. The major difference was that in the first round almost no non-U.S. comments were received, while by 1998 a fifth of comments came from outside the United States. Almost two-thirds of the comments came from individuals, rather than institutions. The existence of the Green Paper had been widely publicized on newsgroups and networks, and while many of the comments were long and thoughtful, most were short. The next largest group was businesses, reflecting the commercial concerns with how the Internet was managed. Perhaps more importantly, non-U.S. entities were more heavily represented among the commenters from institutions, a category that included a diverse group of entities ranging from industry associations through non-governmental organizations and user groups like the Internet Society. This included some of the quasi-official bodies like the Policy Advisory Board, the Policy Oversight Council and the Council of Registrars, all of which were mechanisms set up under the MoU.

A major criticism made of the Green Paper, in many of the comments, was its "U.S.-centric" orientation.

Many commenters noted that the Green Paper largely ignored the work of the CORE in Geneva, proposed a United States location for the central registry corporation and had little role for international organizations. One of the dimensions that Kuhlman and I examined in the comments, was whether the writers saw an international regulatory dimension for the Internet. As can be seen from Table 4.4,[7] most of those who mentioned the international dimension were favorable to it, but commenters from outside the United States were much more likely to both mention and favor an international dimension. This of course included a large number of comments that explicitly favored the CORE

Table 4.3 Type of commenters by origin, March 1998

Type	Non-U.S. (%)	U.S. (%)	Total	Total in %
Academic	9.10	90.90	11	2.1
Business	15.50	84.50	84	16.4
Government	80.00	20.00	5	1.0
Individual	16.00	84.00	326	63.5
Institution	42.90	57.10	49	9.6
Web management	31.60	68.40	38	7.4
Total	20.10	79.90	513	100.0

Table 4.4 Orientation to international governance of the Internet, March 1998 comments

	Non-U.S.	U.S.	Total
Favor	71.8%	40.0%	46.4%
No mention	22.3%	55.4%	48.7%
Oppose	5.8%	4.6%	4.9%
Total	100.0%	100.0%	100.0%
Number	103	410	513

model. In terms of types of commenters, individuals (who were over-whelmingly from the United States) were less likely (44 percent) to mention the international dimension, while institutions (78 percent) and web managers (65 percent) were much more likely to do so.

The United States government took these views into account, to an extent, when they issued their final decision on 5 June 1998, in what was called the White Paper.

The White Paper

The White Paper[8] made few changes to the Green Paper proposals but its basic structure has set the basis for continuing debates about the institutions of Internet governance. It set out four principles to be followed by a new entity in managing the core resources of the Internet.[9]

1 *Stability*   The U.S. government should end its role in the Internet number and name address system in a manner that ensures the stability of the Internet. The introduction of a new management system should not disrupt current operations or create competing root systems. During the transition and thereafter, the stability of the Internet should be the first priority of any DNS management system. Security and reliability of the DNS are important aspects of stability, and as a new DNS management system is introduced, a comprehensive security strategy should be developed.

2 *Competition*   The Internet succeeds in great measure because it is a decentralized system that encourages innovation and maximizes individual freedom. Where possible, market mechanisms that support competition and consumer choice should drive the management of the Internet because they will lower costs, promote innovation, encourage diversity, and enhance user choice and satisfaction.

3 *Private, bottom-up coordination*   Certain management functions require coordination. In these cases, responsible, private sector action is preferable to government control. A private coordinating process is likely to be more flexible than government and to move rapidly enough to meet the changing needs of the Internet and of Internet users. The private process should, as far as possible, reflect the bottom-up governance that has characterized development of the Internet to date.

4 *Representation*   The new corporation should operate as a private entity for the benefit of the Internet community as a whole. The development of sound, fair, and widely accepted policies for the management of DNS will depend on input from the broad and

growing community of Internet users. Management structures should reflect the functional and geographic diversity of the Internet and its users. Mechanisms should be established to ensure international participation in decision-making.

The fourth principle, representation, showed the result of the international comments. In the Green Paper, the last sentence had read "Mechanisms should be established to ensure international input in decision-making," while the final text spoke of "international participation in decision-making." This was a subtle but important shift of emphasis.

In responding to comments on these proposals from the Green Paper, the U.S. government stated that the policy applied only to management of Internet names and addresses and did not set out a "system of Internet 'governance.'" Reacting to concerns about openness, it stated that existing human rights and free speech protections would not be disturbed and, as a result, would not be specifically included in the core principles for DNS management. The policy was not intended to displace other legal regimes like international law, competition law, tax law and principles of international taxation, and intellectual property law that already applied.

The area of trademark disputes, which had been one of the problems that had to be addressed also, was modified between the Green and White papers. The Green Paper only said that trademark disputes should be resolved according to national laws, while the White Paper recognized the role of WIPO in the process, which was requested to initiate a balanced and transparent process, including the participation of trademark holders and members of the Internet community who are not trademark holders, to develop uniform dispute resolution procedures on trademark and intellectual property holders.

The Green Paper had dealt very little with the globalization of the Internet. The White Paper had a major section on the subject, which guided United States policy for almost a decade. The White Paper noted that many comments wanted more globalization of the domain name system, some wanted a larger role for international organizations, some feared that the new arrangement would entrench U.S. control and give it an unfair advantage when new top-level domain names were created. In response, the White Paper stated:

> The U.S. Government believes that the Internet is a global medium and that its technical management should fully reflect the global diversity of Internet users. We recognize the need for and fully support mechanisms that would ensure international input into the

management of the domain name system. In withdrawing the U.S. Government from DNS management and promoting the establishment of a new, non-governmental entity to manage Internet names and addresses, a key U.S. Government objective has been to ensure that the increasingly global Internet user community has a voice in decisions affecting the Internet's technical management.

We believe this process has reflected our commitment. Many of the comments on the Green Paper were filed by foreign entities, including governments. Our dialogue has been open to all Internet users—foreign and domestic, government and private—during this process, and we will continue to consult with the international community as we begin to implement the transition plan outlined in this paper.

ICANN is created

The resulting institution was called the Internet Corporation for Assigned Names and Numbers (ICANN) and was to be a not-for-profit public corporation chartered in California, but with a governance structure—including a board of directors and advisory groups—that would represent all of the key stakeholders. While the U.S. decision maintained the responsibility of the United States government for overseeing the core resources of the Internet, it accepted that this was a shared responsibility and there was an implication that the U.S. oversight function would gradually be removed. California was chosen as a venue because its laws for not-for-profits were fairly flexible and, for legal reasons, ICANN needed a home. By a Memorandum of Understanding with the NTIA, the U.S. government would maintain a formal, but not very active, oversight.

ICANN's evolution is described in Chapter 6. Over the next five years, ICANN functioned reasonably successfully to provide addresses, add new top-level domain names and ensure that the root server system functioned. It was less successful in providing representation to the stakeholders who wanted their interests reflected in ICANN policies and processes. In the meantime, while the critical Internet resources issue was quiet, new policy issues emerged that expanded the need for Internet governance, and it is to these that we must now turn.

5 Regulatory imperatives for Internet governance

Downloading music, free speech, YouTube, porn, and crime and terrorism

Why should the Internet be governed at all? The answer is that a number of issues dealt with elsewhere became important in the Internet. These included issues of intellectual property, freedom of expression and the use of the medium by criminals and for terrorism. Each of these has to be explored to see why there have been incentives to achieve Internet governance.

The Internet became the focus of governmental attention because governments saw reasons to regulate it and because the existing institutions did not seem to work well to deal with problems of order that emerged. If the only issues were architecture or technical standards, the existing institutions would probably have sufficed. And if the regulatory issues having to do with content could be solved by traditional territorial-based institutions, there would be no regulatory imperative for Internet governance. As the Internet has grown, the range of policy issues has expanded as well. The technical bodies described in Chapter 3 were not set up to deal with policy matters. The domain name issue that provoked the creation of ICANN was not really about the protocols on which the Internet was based, but rather on the related issues of sovereignty and intellectual property. Most of the regulatory issues are still unresolved, but almost all have to do with the content that flows over the Internet rather than the channels over which it flows. They really focus on the questions: who owns content and who can regulate it in a borderless world.

Intellectual property

Outside of the unhappiness of many Internet stakeholders in a domain name system essentially run by a private company under contract with a government (Network Solutions and the United States), the main issue provoking the domain name controversy was intellectual property.

The domain registrars did not check whether the domains that they registered were trademarked by anyone. Indeed, if only national laws were to be applied, there could be conflicting trademarks, so long as they did not exist in the same geographical space. An example is Budweiser beer. The brand name was trademarked in the United States and most other countries by the Anheuser-Busch Corporation. But in the Czech Republic the trademark was held by the *Budejovicky Budvar* Corporation. The two had argued about this for a century, but so long as one company's beer was not sold in the other company's country, the dispute was resolvable, although a century's worth of litigation was clearly good for the legal profession.

Pokey and the madonna.com problem

The borderless Internet effectively eliminated territorial solutions. There could only be one trademark holder in cyberspace, but the question was, whose trademark would prevail? In some cases, the resolution was achieved by the parties concerned. A famous case had to do with a young boy who had been given the nickname "Pokey" by his parents. He registered a domain as pokey.org. However, Pokey was also a character in an animated television program called Gumby, and the producers of the program had trademarked all of the names. Lawyers for the producers sent the 12-year-old boy a cease and desist letter. This reached the newspapers and the resultant bad publicity led the producers to accept the legitimacy of Pokey the boy's claim to pokey.com.[1] Others who registered domain names were not so innocent. Some saw registration of domain names as a means of obtaining money from trademark holders who might want them for their own web sites. This practice is called "cybersquatting" and became a major annoyance. One of the motivations behind the MoUtld that sparked the domain name controversy was to eliminate cybersquatting by placing dispute resolution with the World Intellectual Property Organization. The ICANN agreement included setting up a UDRP (Uniform Dispute Resolution Process), whereby disputes about ownership of domain names could be resolved through an agreed process. One of the main UDRPs is administered by WIPO. From 1999 to September 2007 it considered 11,837 complaints covering 21,594 domain names.[2] The dispute resolution process consists of WIPO appointing a neutral panelist to weigh the competing claims and determine who should have the domain name.

One of the cases that has been frequently cited in the WIPO proceedings was lodged by Madonna Ciccone, who sings under the name

Madonna, against Dan Parisi. Parisi had registered the domain name madonna.com (along with some 600 other domain names including whitehouse.com). Parisi was considered one of the archetypical cybersquatters, who would agree to give up the domain name in exchange for a fee. Madonna appealed to the WIPO UDRP (Case D2000–0847) and won on the grounds that she had a greater claim to the name. The domain madonna.com was transferred to her.

As Christopher May put it in one of the companion volumes of the Global Institutions series, WIPO has had a rise, a fall and a comeback.[3] The fall was when the World Trade Organization adopted agreements on trade-related aspects of intellectual property rights (TRIPS), essentially making WIPO the secondary player, and the comeback was fueled by the Internet. The debate about enforcing intellectual property is intimately connected with Internet governance, although this is not formally recognized. In fact, the outcome documents of WSIS only mention intellectual property twice, both in the context of its earlier Geneva phase (see Chapter 7). The Tunis phase studiously ignored the term, largely because industrialized countries wanted to keep it in WIPO and WTO, where they perceived they have more influence.

Downloading, Kazaa, MySpace and YouTube

While domain names involved some money and considerable annoyance to large companies, the real intellectual property issues on the Internet have to do with downloadable content, especially music and movies. As soon as it was possible to digitalize music files, as is done on compact disks (CDs), it was possible to share them over the Internet. The issue of sharing music had been taken up before, when tape recording technology had advanced to permit individuals to copy music from their vinyl records to tape. In theory, the same record could have been copied multiple times and given to friends, or even sold. This did not concern the recording industry because the quality of the copied music was not as good as the original record. Similarly, when movies were sold on videotape, they also could be copied. A court case in the United States in 1984 resolved the matter for some time. In Sony Corp. of America vs. Universal City Studios, Inc., called the "Betamax Case," the United States Supreme Court ruled that the making of individual copies of complete television shows for purposes of time-shifting does not constitute copyright infringement, but is fair use. The court also ruled that the manufacturers of home video recording devices, such as Betamax or other VCRs, cannot be liable for infringement.

The case was a boon to the home video market as it created a legal safe haven for the technology, which also significantly benefited the entertainment industry through the sale of pre-recorded movies.[4] This solved the problem, even when music (and movies) moved to digital media (compact disks or CD-ROMs). It was easier to make copies of the content with almost the same quality as the original. An industry of pirated CDs developed in some countries, but this also could be dealt with through normal procedures. For example, the entry of China into the World Trade Organization was delayed until that country agreed to crack down on pirated software, music and movies (and demonstrated a willingness to actually do so). The Russian Federation's application for the WTO is also being delayed until that country agrees to deal with pirating.

Internet technology soon made the normal arrangements obsolete. Digitalized content can be transmitted over the Internet using standard packet-switching technology. CDs and DVDs can be copied onto computer hard drives and then sent over the Internet. If this is done for commercial purposes, as is the case with commercial services like Apple's iTunes, this does not represent a problem, since fees to copyright holders can be included in the cost of the download and digital rights management (DRM) software can prevent excessive copying. There are two methods for supplying content: either the content can be stored on a central server and then downloaded, or the content can be stored on individual computers and then transferred to other computers over the Internet. This latter is called peer-to-peer sharing (P2P). Server-based sharing can be controlled, since if the content violates intellectual property rules, the IP owner can be sued in national jurisdictions. However, P2P sharing raises essential issues of fair use. At what point does fair use end and violation of intellectual property rights begin?

The notion held by some of the initial providers of downloadable music was that once an individual had bought, say, a CD, he or she could share it with friends. The "friends" could be other unknown users of the Internet, often known by anonymous pseudonyms. If software was available, one could access the computer of a friend like "bobdylanfan" and download the music files resident on his hard disk. Companies like gnutella.com provided P2P software. When I quiz my graduate students—over 70 percent of whom are not from the United States—about whether they have downloaded music without paying for it, almost all of them say that they have.

The efforts of the music industry through the Recording Industry Association of America (RIAA) to control downloadable music indicate the nature of the problem. The RIAA sues downloaders and companies providing either servers or software in the United States. But if the downloaders are located outside the United States, it is difficult and costly to make them liable. There are a number of famous cases that illustrate the problem. Sharman Systems, a corporation providing both server space and software for sharing music using a software called KaZaA, was sued by the RIAA because it enabled peer-to-peer sharing of music. An article in the *New York Times* described RIAA's problem:[5]

> Having vanquished the music swapping service Napster in court, the entertainment industry is facing a formidable obstacle in pursuing its major successor, KaZaA: geography.
>
> Sharman Networks, the distributor of the program, is incorporated in the South Pacific island nation of Vanuatu and managed from Australia. Its computer servers are in Denmark and the source code for its software was last seen in Estonia.
>
> KaZaA's original developers, who still control the underlying technology, are thought to be living in the Netherlands—although entertainment lawyers seeking to have them charged with violating United States copyright law have been unable to find them.
>
> What KaZaA has in the United States are users—millions of them—downloading copyrighted music, television shows and movies 24 hours a day.

When the lawsuit began, Sharman Systems had been operating out of San Diego, California, but the owners quickly moved their business to Australia. Eventually, Universal Music, which has an Australian affiliate, sued Sharman Systems there and, in 2005, won a case, but only after winning another case in the United States. As an analysis of the Australian case put it:[6]

> On the heels of the decision of the U.S. Supreme Court in *MGM Studios v. Grokster*, 125 S. Ct. 2764 (2005), where the Court found that file-sharing services could be held liable for contributory copyright infringement, the Federal Court of Australia on September 5th decided *Universal Music Australia Pty Ltd. v. Sharman License Holdings Ltd.*, [2005] FCA 1242. Justice Wilcox of the Federal Court held that certain defendants associated with Sharman Networks were liable for "authorization" of copyright infringement as a result of having distributed the Kazaa file-sharing software.

There is a long list of individual cases where content owners have tried to recover damages from up- or downloaders. This included the famous case where a Russian programmer was arrested while attending a conference in the United States and charged with violating a United States law, the 1998 Digital Millennium Copyright Act, for writing software in Russia that was not illegal there.[7] The programmer, Dmitry Sklyarov, was defended by the Electronic Frontier Foundation, and, in December 2002, was found not guilty by a jury in San Jose, California.

The number of cases has been increasing over time, as new Internet technologies come into use. The ability of individuals to upload videos that they have made themselves onto what are called "social networking" sites like MySpace and YouTube, has led to cases where copyright owners have sought to have content taken down as violating their copyrights. As the Internet becomes a major source of news and information, the issue is likely to increase in importance.

Public domain and freedom of expression

As a matter of Internet governance, the regulation of intellectual property turns on what is called "fair use." In intellectual property law, copyrights are supposed to be time-limited and there is a principle of fair use, that copies can be made without violating the law, up to a certain point. The examples usually given are quotations from a book used in a review (or in this book) or the copying of an article by a professor to use in a class.[8] The Internet, however, makes fair use highly ambiguous since, if an excerpt is posted on a website, it is available to everyone on the planet who has an Internet connection and a search engine.

Fair use in the Internet age has not been defined, and is subject to considerable debate. Some content owners find it useful to give permission for their material to be freely available, because it probably means that many of those who download a text will decide to purchase it later. Other content owners are jealous of their rights and seek to prevent downloading. A recent case is the dispute between Apple Computer, whose iTunes has been a remarkably successful (and profitable) form of downloading, and recording companies. Apple provides downloading of individual music tracks for a fee, but until recently the tracks contained software that prevented easy duplication of the music. This software, called Digital Rights Management (DRM) software was used as an argument, in France, for why Apple was engaging in monopolistic practices under European law. The CEO of Apple, Steve Jobs, wrote an article arguing that DRM should not be used because it was a flawed and expensive business model.[9]

One problem that has been noted is that many musicians, for example, do not own the copyright to their music, having sold the publishing rights as a means of supporting themselves while they became popular. An example in the pre-Internet era was a US Federal Court case entitled *Fantasy vs. Fogerty*, 510 U.S. 517 (1994). The singer and composer John Fogerty of the band Creedence Clearwater Revival, had written a song called "Run through the Jungle" that he had sold to his record company, Fantasy Records. He subsequently left the band and began a solo career and wrote another song, "Old Man Down the Road," that Fantasy claimed was the same as "Run Through the Jungle" and therefore violated its copyright. In the trial, the jury ruled that it was not copyright infringement, noting that both songs were written by the same person.[10]

The ability of musicians to distribute their music directly over the Internet puts a new dimension to fair use. A number of non-governmental organizations have been formed to promote an international approach to this issue. One is IP Justice, "an international civil liberties organization that promotes balanced intellectual property law."[11] The Executive Director of the NGO, Robin Gross, is an attorney who began as a staff attorney with the Electronic Frontier Foundation.

While much of the public focus has been on music, videos and movies as intellectual property issues, an additional source of focus is on freedom of expression more broadly, in terms of the right of governments to block Internet content that might otherwise be available to their citizens. The earliest examples of these included a case where Compuserve, an early Internet service provider that had an office in Germany, was prosecuted by the German government because users could access sites in the Netherlands that contained what the government considered hate propaganda. A more recent example was the successful effort by the government of China to have search engines operating in the country, including Google and Yahoo, systematically block certain sites considered by the government to be harmful.

Critics of these approaches have argued that the essential value of the Internet is its openness. Vint Cerf, in an interview with the BBC after the U.K.'s Conservative Party floated ideas to curb the access of British youth to sites such as YouTube that let them see videos showing extreme or callous violence, affirmed that:[12]

> he rejected calls for strict control of what is put online. He said the net was just a reflection of the society in which we live. Anyone regulating beyond what was clearly illegal put themselves on a "slippery slope" that could limit freedom of expression, he said.

"If it's not illegal, it raises a rather interesting question about where you do draw the line," he said.

One factor at play in this discussion is that political speech is protected under the Universal Declaration on Human Rights, to which all states have subscribed. Article 19 of the Declaration states:

Everyone has the right to freedom of opinion and expression; this right includes freedom to hold opinions without interference and to seek, receive and impart information and ideas through any media and regardless of frontiers.

To a certain extent, that was more theoretical than real until the Internet made all information and ideas that are transmitted through it available to everyone.

Porn

The issue of freedom of expression, and its regulation, in the Internet is most clearly drawn in the area of pornography. There is no universal definition of what constitutes pornography. In a United States Supreme Court decision on a case where the manager of a cinema was prosecuted for showing what was considered a pornographic film (*Jacobellis vs. Ohio*, 378 U.S. 184 (1964)), the court held that the film in question was not obscene. In a concurring opinion, Justice Potter Stewart famously stated "I shall not today attempt further to define the kinds of material I understand to be embraced within that shorthand description; and perhaps I could never succeed in intelligibly doing so. But I know it when I see it and the motion picture involved in this case is not that."

The problem is that community standards differ from place to place within countries and even more greatly between countries. The transmission of pornographic content is one of the major businesses of the Internet, with the sites usually located in countries whose standard is less strict. It is therefore almost impossible for a country that prohibits or limits sexual content to prevent access to that content over the Internet. As long as at least one country does not prohibit the content, servers could be set up there to provide the content.

There is one exception to this rule and that is child pornography, defined as any representation, by whatever means, of a child engaged in real or simulated explicit sexual activities or any representation of the sexual parts of a child for primarily sexual purposes. There is a universal agreement that this is prohibited speech, and this agreement is reflected in the Optional Protocol to the Convention on the Rights of the Child on the Sale of Children, Child Prostitution and Child Pornography adopted by the United Nations on 25 May 2000. States party to the protocol are expected, as a minimum, to criminalize "Producing, distributing, disseminating, importing, exporting, offering, selling or possessing for the above purposes child pornography." As of October 2007, 123 countries are party to the protocol. However, child pornography could still be transmitted from countries that are not party to the protocol.

Crime and terrorism

A similar situation occurs with regard to crime and terrorism over the Internet. Governments have expressed concern that non-state actors engaged in terrorism use the Internet to communicate with each other and to spread their ideas. Al-Qaida, which has taken credit for the attack on the United States on 11 September 2001, has used Internet sites to issue proclamations, usually using software tools like anonymizers (which hide the source of transmission) and by closing down sites before they can be located.

One problem with terrorism is that it has not been defined, so that a person or group considered in one country to be a terrorist can be considered a resistance fighter by another country. While there are a large number of international conventions covering terrorist acts, like hijacking aircraft, financing terrorist organizations and taking hostages, none of these apply to information and communication. There is no agreement about what content can be considered "terrorist." Given this ambiguity, it is difficult to stop groups from using the Internet to transmit content.

Another issue is spamming, the abuse of electronic messaging systems to indiscriminately send unsolicited bulk messages. To be able to do this, spammers have to be able to access e-mail addresses, often by using what are called "bots" (short for web robots, software applications that run automated tasks over the Internet). Bots harvest e-mail addresses and these are used to send spam, the unsolicited content. Some of the spam is vaguely commercial, while some of it involves criminal activities. Examples include messages sent from Nigeria (and other countries) seeking partners to retrieve money supposedly lodged in banks by former heads of state (or persons killed in plane crashes without heirs).

Another form of crime is what is called phishing. This involves using e-mail or instant messaging to fool persons into providing banking information, including account numbers and passwords, that would allow the phishers to access the accounts.

Both spamming and phishing undermine the confidence people have in electronic communication, as well as using critical resources. They are related to a security issue, denial of service attacks, that also use bots and other software tools to overwhelm servers and web sites with information requests so as to disable them. This is been practiced on a number of occasions, against both government web sites and private ones. One of the most dramatic instances was a denial of service attack on web sites and servers in Estonia, allegedly in response to relocation of a war memorial, that sought to shut down government and political party sites.[13]

More importantly, there is no agreement on where liability for content rests. Some governments want to hold the ISPs responsible, and if content prohibited by the government passes through the ISP servers, they are liable. Others take the position that it is the sender of the message that is liable rather than the channel used. As noted in Chapter 3, this is an old and unresolved issue that began with hacking. However, one approach, favored in Western developed countries, is reflected in the Convention on Cybercrime adopted by the Council of Europe. This is to require the service provider to disclose the source of what is deemed illegal content to government authorities.[14]

One difficulty with the Cybercrime Convention is that it was negotiated by a non-universal body and its states party consist almost completely of members of the Council of Europe and not all of them have ratified the treaty. In fact, as of October 2007, only 21 states were party to the treaty, while another 22 had signed it without ratifying. The only non-member of the Council of Europe to become a party was the United States. Thus, the reach of its provisions is not very broad and many would argue that a universal agreement would be necessary to address cybercrime effectively.

There are the beginnings of an international agreement, however, that dealing with cybersecurity and crime is an international responsibility. The International Telecommunications Union states:[15]

> that with the application and development of information and communication technologies (ICTs), new threats from various sources have emerged that may have an impact on confidence and security in the use of ICTs ... and on the preservation of peace and the economic and social development of all Member States, and that threats to and vulnerabilities of networks continue to give rise to evergrowing security challenges across national borders for all countries, in particular developing countries.

In order to deal with the problem, the ITU called for coordinated national action for prevention, preparation, response and recovery from an incident. A key element of the ITU policy is the need to involve government authorities, the private sector, citizens and users, as well as international secretariats.

This is part of a broader recognition that solutions to the problems described in this chapter need the cooperation of governments, the private sector and civil society if they are to be effective. This multi-stakeholder model has been put into place in two places where it emerged, in the ICANN, set up to govern the critical Internet resources, and in the World Summit for the Information Society, to which we will now turn.

6 The ICANN experiment

The creation of the Internet Corporation for Assigned Names and Numbers (ICANN) on 18 September 1998 was the immediate consequence of the governance issue described in Chapter 4. It describes itself[1] as follows:

> ICANN is the international non-profit, multi-stakeholder organization that is the globally authoritative body to coordinate the Internet systems of Unique Identifiers, including to ensure the stability and interoperability of those Identifiers.

ICANN was considered by its founders to be an experiment in a new type of governance institution that would essentially be non-governmental. As the White Paper put it,[2]

> The policy that follows does not propose a monolithic structure for Internet governance. We doubt that the Internet should be governed by one plan or one body or even by a series of plans and bodies. Rather, we seek a stable process to address the narrow issues of management and administration of Internet names and numbers on an ongoing basis.
>
> As set out below, the U.S. Government is prepared to recognize, by entering into agreement with, and to seek international support for, a new, not-for-profit corporation formed by private sector Internet stakeholders to administer policy for the Internet name and address system. Under such agreement(s) or understanding(s), the new corporation would undertake various responsibilities for the administration of the domain name system now performed by or on behalf of the U.S. Government or by third parties under arrangements or agreements with the U.S. Government.

ICANN has evolved into a unique international organization for regulating critical Internet resources, but has remained controversial since, for many netizens, it reflects a dominance of the private sector and is not transparent, and for many governments still has unacceptable connections to the United States government. Its evolution, trying to deal with the four principles that were to guide it—stability, competition, private bottom-up coordination, and representation—has conditioned how the broader issues of Internet governance are being approached. Over the nine years since its creation, ICANN has sought to provide the alternative means of Internet core resource governance that were envisaged for it, with only limited success and continued controversy.

ICANN as an international institution

While recognizing that ICANN is an international institution, it is formally a not-for-profit corporation chartered in the state of California. California—a location that was selected for its rather flexible laws concerning not-for-profit corporations and, probably, the fact that it was a center of information technology development. It was also the home of Jon Postel, the founder of IANA, a function taken over by ICANN.

There are precedents for international institutions that function as private entities while providing public services, but none as radical in design as ICANN. The International Organization for Standardization (ISO), as an example, was set up to reach agreements on international standards (desirable characteristics of products and services such as quality, environmental friendliness, safety, reliability, efficiency, and interchangeability—and at an economical cost).[3] The ISO is composed of 157 national standards institutes, one per country, some of which are governmental and some of which are private sector. As a result, ISO considers itself a non-governmental organization even though it is heavily governmental. In the development of standards, ISO is similar to the IETF, working through technical committees (some 193 in 2007) governed by a Technical Management Board made up of representatives from national affiliates.

The authority of ICANN goes beyond that of ISO and similar institutions in that ICANN can make binding decisions on Internet architecture and policies for domain names. It does not make decisions, like most international organizations or technical bodies like the IETF, by consensus, but rather by vote. For that reason, individuals that participate in its governance structure have always been seen as more important than for earlier Internet institutions.

Evolution of governance

Milton Mueller describes the origins of ICANN as a political process that sought a consensus among some of the main players in the domain name dispute.[4] These included the technical community, large businesses (especially IBM and MCI), the Internet Society, the European Union, and international organizations like ITU and WIPO. They worked with the Clinton administration to craft the White Paper Agreement. Translating the agreement into an institution essentially played insiders against almost insiders.

The White Paper had called for private initiatives to create the new institution. As Mueller recounts it, the first initiative was organized by Anthony Rutkowski as a Global Incorporation Alliance Workshop, which was later named the Internet Forum on the White Paper (IFWP). This was intended to bring in both the private sector and civil society in an open dialogue. Rutkowski had been involved with the Internet for some time, first as a lawyer for the U.S. federal government, then as legal counsel for the International Telecommunications Union, and then as executive secretary of the Internet Society. He had developed an antipathy for government, international organizations, and the technical community during his service and had become a consultant for Network Solutions.

On the other side were the technical elite, led by Jon Postel, who had been running IANA since its beginning. He had organized an IANA Transition Advisory Group made up of colleagues who had been running the Internet addressing machinery. Postel hired a lawyer with Washington connections to draw up articles of incorporation and bylaws for the new corporation. As Mueller notes,[5]

> It would incorporate under California law as a non-profit public benefit corporation, a structure typically used for educational and charitable organizations. Half of the board would be self-selected by the initial board members. The other half would be appointed by functional constituencies called Supporting Organizations. Two of the three Supporting Organizations (addresses and protocols) would be controlled by the technical community. The composition of the third Supporting Organization, devoted to domain names, was not specified, but presumably was intended to represent business and user stakeholders in line with the criteria of the White Paper.

The two processes, the open one organized by IFWP and the more closed one organized by IANA, occasionally overlapped and the IFWP was routinely attended by people connected with IANA. The IFWP process discussions were leading to a different type of organizational model, one which, as Mueller put it, would be[6]

> a non-profit, membership-based organization managed and controlled by an elected board representing various interest groups. This model was based on the assumption that the participants in the new organization would serve not because they were altruistic, but in order to advance their business, professional, or personal interests; hence, the organization was set up like a business corporation that substituted members for shareholders.

These were clearly alternative views, which have competed over time. Postel's was more like the IETF model, while the IFWP was more like a trade association. They gave different weights to different stakeholders. One of the players in the negotiations was Network Solutions, which had the most to lose financially from any new organization that did not maintain its monopoly on non-governmental top-level domain names.

The White Paper had called for a consensus-based approach to defining the new institution, but despite efforts, the competing interests were not willing to compromise. A key issue was the position of Network Solutions. The groups that favored the MoUtld agreement did not want to confirm Network Solutions, while Network Solutions did not wish to relinquish its monopoly. There were disagreements about how to elect members of the board of directors and how the board would make decisions.

The matter was resolved by the United States government, which decided to accept the proposal of the Postel group to create ICANN. The Commerce Department entered into a Memorandum of Understanding with ICANN to manage the root and ICANN subsequently entered into an agreement with the University of Southern California to take over the IANA functions.

As a consequence of the process, ICANN makes decisions by vote and election to its board is contentious. The process also guaranteed that ICANN would be fraught with controversy.

Initial setup

Following the architecture proposed by Postel's group, ICANN was incorporated in California and its initial board of directors was essentially self-appointed. It consisted of nine members plus the president of ICANN. The interim board was carefully balanced (Table 6.1). Half of the members were from the United States. Three were from Europe and two from Asia. There were three women. Three were from universities, while the rest were from business. The board included known Internet pioneers like Jun Murai from Japan.

The position of chair of the board was given to an icon, Esther Dyson. Dyson is a venture capitalist and writer, who was chair of the Electronic Frontier Foundation from 1995 to 1998 and thus involved in the Internet freedom movement. In an article that she posted in her online journal, RELease 1.0, Dyson said of the EFF, "the basic message of the Foundation is, 'There's a new world coming. Let's make sure it has rules we can live with.' These rules will establish the rights and also the responsibilities of the users of the electronic infrastructure—which means, eventually, all of us."[7]

The selection for first president and chief executive officer of ICANN was equally symbolic. The choice, pushed by the IANA group as well as the Department of Commerce, was Michael M. Roberts. Roberts came from the academic community, where he had been Stanford University's Deputy Director of Information Technology Services, with executive responsibilities in Stanford's computing, communications, and information systems programs. He had then gone on to become vice president at EDUCOM, a consortium of 600 universities and colleges with interests in information technology, where he was responsible for networking and telecommunications programs, including the development of public policy positions in information technology on behalf of EDUCOM members.[8] The intent was to establish ICANN as more of an academic than a business organization.

Half of the initial board members exited in 2000, including Dyson, while the rest were all gone by 2003. This reflected both the evolution and the controversy generated by ICANN.

ICANN had to deal with a number of critical issues at the outset. It had to set up the Supporting Organizations that would provide the remainder of the board members, including elections. It had to deal with the issues of intellectual property that had provoked the first Internet crisis described in Chapter 4. It had to decide how to allocate registry positions, both for top-level domains like .com and .org, and for country-level domain names, and it had to decide on new top-level domains to increase the number of names that could be used. It also had to figure out how to fund the organization until it could produce its own revenue.[9]

The first two and a half years of operation, to 2001, saw decision-making based on finding middle grounds that would satisfy main stakeholders, although no decisions probably satisfied all of them. To deal with the intellectual property problem, ICANN set up the Universal Dispute Resolution Policy (UDRP). This was largely based on consultations

Table 6.1 Initial members of the ICANN board of directors

Member	Nationality	Current position	Sex	International experience	Member until
Geraldine Capdeboscq	France	Executive Vice President for Strategy, Technology and Partnerships, BULL	F	European ICT	2000
George Conrades	U.S.A.	Chairman and Chief Executive Officer of Akamai Technologies, Inc.	M	IBM	2000
Greg Crew	Australia	Chair of AITEC Ltd. and ASCA21 Pty. Ltd, and a director of ERG Ltd.	M	Asia business	2000
Esther Dyson	U.S.A.	Venture capitalist with connections to Electronic Frontier Foundation	F	Internet civil society	2000
Frank Fitzsimmons	U.S.A.	Chief Operating Officer for Iridian Technologies	M	International business	2002
Hans Kraaijenbrink	Netherlands	Executive Board of ETNO, the European Telecommunications Network Operators association	M	European ICT	2003
Jun Murai	Japan	Professor, Faculty of Environmental Information, Keio University	M	United Nations University	2003
Michael M. Roberts	U.S.A.	President and CEO of ICANN	M	Vice President at EDUCOM, a consortium of 600 universities and colleges with interests in information technology	2001
Eugenio Triana	Spain	International management consultant on telecom policy, space and satellite systems, copyright and intellectual property rights	M	European ICT	2000
Linda S. Wilson	U.S.A.	President emerita of Radcliffe College	F	U.S. education and government	2003

undertaken by WIPO that involved the main stakeholders in the global intellectual property system. It involved allowing open access to a database on contact information for domain name registrants (the WHOIS database), developing procedures that would allow trademark and copyright holders to protest use by others and setting up a procedure for arbitration when names conflicted. The initial proposals by WIPO were resisted by a combination of domain name registries, the Internet Society and others in the technical community and civil liberties groups who felt that the proposals were too restrictive. The final proposals that were adopted in 1999 were also based on WIPO's consultations but provided for a number of possible arbitration panels other than WIPO itself. The resulting system, as noted in Chapter 5, seems to work well.

To deal with competition in registration of domain names, ICANN had to find a way to allow other registries to operate while, because of U.S. domestic politics, maintaining Network Solutions' role. The resulting system allowed competition among registrars for .com domains, while allowing Network Solutions (acquired by Verisign Corporation in 2000 and then privatized in 2003) to be the main "wholesaler," charging the registries a fee, set at $9 per registration, determined by the United States Department of Commerce, for including domains in the root. The solution really pleased no-one but has continued to the present day.

Funding ICANN was an initial problem, since the intention was to assess registrars with a fee to be recognized. An initial proposal was to charge registrars a fixed fee of $5,000 plus a fee of $1 per year per domain name registration. The cost would be built into the registrar's fee to consumers. Many of the registries thought the ICANN fee to be too high and objected, working through the United States Congress, which put pressure on ICANN. Eventually, the financing system was put in place after ICANN reached an agreement with Network Solutions. By 2007, ICANN functioned on the basis of income from registrations (at $0.20 per registration) and from registrars of the top-level domain names for its $49 million budget. ICANN is exploring how to obtain resources from country-code registrars that, up to now, have not been willing to become invested in the organization. Figure 6.1 shows the distribution of revenues in 2007.

The first elections

A major feature of the start-up of ICANN was completing the board of directors. The original by-laws, adopted when the corporation was established, called for a board of between 9 and 18 members. The initial nine members had essentially been self-selected, so one of the first

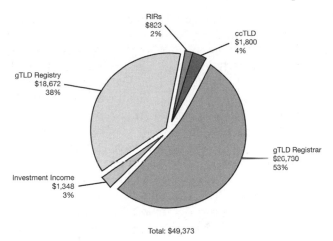

RIRs
$823
2%

ccTLD
$1,800
4%

gTLD Registry
$18,672
38%

gTLD Registrar
$20,730
53%

Investment Income
$1,348
3%

Total: $49,373

Figure 6.1 Sources of revenue for ICANN, 2007–8.
Source: ICANN, approved budget fiscal 2007–8, 29 June 2007, p. 19.

institutional matters to address was filling out the board. In addition to the nine at-large positions, the original by-laws provided for three members each from three Supporting Organizations. These began to organize themselves.

The first was the Protocol Supporting Organization. This was intended to ensure that ICANN did not adopt addressing protocols that deviated from the global consensus. As a result, the proposal for the organization was initiated in the IETF. The organization was essentially run by the IETF techies, who nominated three members for the board. They included two European technical managers, Jean-François Abramatic who was the chair of the W3C Consortium and Phillip Davidson, a senior manager for British Telecom. The third member elected by the Protocol Supporting Organization was Vint Cerf, one of the "fathers of the Internet."

The second was the Address Supporting Organization. According to the ICANN by-laws, the ASO was formally intended to have responsibility for defining global policies for the distribution and registration of Internet address space (currently IPv4 and IPv6, for the distribution and registration of identifiers used in Internet inter-domain routing (currently BGP autonomous system numbers)) and other parts of the DNS space, as well as to advise on the operation of the DNS root name servers for these spaces.

The ASO was to be made up of the regional Internet registries, charged with "providing Internet resource allocations, registration services and co-ordination activities that support the operation of the Internet globally."[10] At the time there were three, ARIN (North and South America), RIPE NCC (Europe), and APNIC (Asia and the Pacific), to be joined later by AfriNIC (Africa). The ASO elected three directors, all non-U.S., one for each region. For ARIN, the director was Ken Fockler, an IP attorney from Canada. The director for RIPE NCC was Robert Blokzijil, the RIPE chairman from the Netherlands. And the director for APNIC was Pindar Wong, a businessman from Hong Kong who was chairman of the Asia & Pacific Internet Association.

The third organization was the Domain Name Supporting Organization (DNSO). Unlike the PSO and the ASO, the DNSO (like most international organizations, ICANN is afflicted with acronymitis), was not easy to create. It was expected to reflect the views of the other constituencies with which ICANN was supposed to consult. This was a highly diverse set of stakeholders, consisting of all other groups that were users of the Internet. When trying to establish the DNSO, ICANN listed six constituencies including registries, registrars, commercial and business entities, ISPs and connectivity providers, intellectual property interests, and non-commercial domain name holders.[11]

The DNSO constituencies met in Berlin in May 1999. They agreed to establish a Names Council to conduct business, including determining the directors. The Names Council would have three members from each of the recognized constituencies, although even this was contentious since it was argued that the gTLD registries were already represented through the ASO.

During 1999–2002, the Names Council met, according to its statistics, 64 times with its chair rotating among different constituency groups.[12] The problem was that there was no formal mechanism for the constituencies to agree. The constituting document of the DNSO stated that decisions should be reached by consensus, brokered by the Names Council. However, even the composition of constituency groups, like the non-commercial domain name holders (essentially, the civil society and educational users) was contentious until the ICANN board itself decided on how to recognize them. Eventually, the Names Council met by teleconference on 5 October 1999, facilitated by the Berkman Center at Harvard University, which had become interested in Internet governance. As the report of the meeting noted, "Jonathan Zittrain and his students will work on pro bono effort (no cost, educational experience for Harvard students) with the NC, trying to formalise adequate procedures adapted for the DNSO needs."[13]

The council agreed to have proxy voting over the Internet to elect the ICANN directors that would be provided by DNSO. Each of the members of the Names Council could vote for up to three candidates from among the nominees. A set of rules was agreed based on what was called "convention-style voting."[14] For this, nominees would be presented to the Names Council, whose members would each vote for one. The council would get a ranked list and the nominee with the lowest number of votes (including none) would be eliminated and there would be other rounds of voting until a nominee received a majority of votes. A similar process is applied in the United Nations General Assembly for contested elections. For the first election this process was applied for three nominees, one to have a three-year term, another a two-year and one only a one-year term.

There were 14 nominated candidates and the election proceeded in an orderly fashion. The three winners came from different constituencies. Alejandro Pisanty, Director of Computing Academic Services at the National Autonomous University of Mexico, was also the head of Mexico's Internet Society. Amadeu Abril i Abril was a lawyer who taught European Union law, competition law, and IT law at ESADE Law School, Ramon Lull University in Spain, who had also been involved in the gTLD-MoU Policy Oversight Committee. Jonathan Cohen was a Canadian intellectual property lawyer who had been involved in WIPO. Of the 11 non-elected nominated candidates, three (Karl Auerbach, Peter Dengate-Thrush, and Nii Quaynor) were later elected to the board.

The openness of the process was notable for international organizations and was consistent with ICANN's mandate to be transparent.

The final element in the construction of a decision-making body was the replacement of the self-appointed board members by members who would be elected at-large. There were few precedents for a global election of individuals to serve as on the executive of an international organization. In intergovernmental organizations, the main mechanism was a geographical apportionment of seats and then having regional groups of countries determine who they would nominate. Only if a regional group fails to agree on a slate of candidates does the election become contested. In the private sector, the board of directors usually presents its slate of candidates to the stockholders. Elections are only contested if there is an opposing slate.

The ICANN board spent much of 1999 trying to devise a mechanism for electing at-large members. As described by Mueller, the process was difficult.[15] The board appointed a Membership Advisory Committee chaired by Greg Crew and including Diane Cabell from the Berkman Center and Izumi Aizu of Japan, who made a set of radical proposals, including the notion that the at-large members should be elected by individual voters. The at-large members would elect five board members on a regional basis and four on a global basis. The board found this procedure too complex to endorse. They found the proposals complex and expensive and discovered that individual members, under the California law that governed ICANN, could have the right to inspect books and go to the courts. They tried to set up an indirect election based on an "at-large council," but this met resistance and in the end the board agreed that, in 2000, five board members would be elected from regional groups. The Markle Foundation, headed by the politically connected lawyer Zoë Baird, provided funding for the election. The process required individuals to sign up as at-large members of ICANN, which 158,000 did, of which 76,502 activated their memberships in time to be eligible and 34,035 actually voted.

The board set up a nominating committee to propose candidates, but others could be nominated by members. In the end, the nominating committee provided 18 nominees divided among the five regions, while an additional nine nominees came directly from the members. Among those nominated by ICANN was Lawrence Lessig, who, as noted in Chapter 5, was a critical specialist in intellectual property.

There was, however, widespread dissatisfaction with the board and its apparent lack of transparency. This had been building since the White Paper. A number of non-governmental activists from the United States, Korea, Japan, England, Germany, France, and Australia joined in a loose coalition to promote a common agenda. Together they launched the Civil Society Internet Forum (CSIF) as a collective framework for participation in the elections. As described by Hans Klein, one of its founders, in an article analyzing the election,[16]

> The CSIF articulated a collective platform in its "Civil Society Statement." During the summer of 2000 some of the leading NGO activists and election candidates (especially Karl Auerbach, who later won the North American election) composed this document, which stated principles for governance and derived from them a series of concrete reforms for ICANN.

The voting was outsourced to a company that ran online elections, but the results were, as Mueller put it, "stunning." In Europe and North America, the candidates proposed by the nominating committee lost badly. Karl Auerbach, who had been involved in the Berkman Center's work and was known as a free Internet advocate and had been an unsuccessful candidate from the DNSO, won the North American election on the reform platform. He became a gadfly on the ICANN board, even suing ICANN, with the help of the Electronic Frontier Foundation, to obtain access to corporate documents. The European winner was Andy Mueller-Maguhn, whom one reporter characterized as "a student of information science at the Free University of Berlin and member of the infamous Hamburg Chaos Computer Club, which stands for unlimited freedom and flow of information without censorship."[17] The second-place finisher in the European region was Jeannette Hoffman, a researcher at the Social Science Research Center Berlin (WZB) where she was the head of the "Internet and Policy" project. Hoffman subsequently became a partner in the Internet Governance Project and a member of the Multistakeholder Advisory Committee described in Chapter 8.

The other three winners were proposed by the nominating committee. Masanobu Katoh from Japan was an executive of Fujitsu who had been active in the DNSO. Ivan Moura Campos of Brazil was CEO of Akwan Information Technologies and chairman of the Internet Steering Committee of Brazil. And finally, Nii Quaynor from Ghana had been active in the DNSO and had established the computer science department at the University of Cape-Coast in Ghana. He had considerable experience with the United Nations as a member of the secretary-general's Advisory Group on ICT, chair of the OAU Internet Task Force, chairman of the AfriNIC, member of the Worldbank Infodev TAP, member of the ITU Telecom board, president of the Internet Society of Ghana, and member of the council of the University of Ghana.

The first fully elected board was therefore constituted. The process, however, was rocky and as a result changes were made for subsequent elections. The DNSO, as originally conceived, was much too heterogeneous to provide input and the at-large election process was perceived to be too complex. Hans Klein reflected on the process and concluded:[18]

> The ICANN elections do not support the strongest scepticism about the feasibility of global democracy. Those elections provided evidence of all four preconditions of democracy [a membership, a communication capability, a system of interest aggregation, and a democratic culture]. They cast doubt on the sceptics' strong claim that realizing the preconditions of democracy is *absolutely* impossible at the global level. However, one cannot conclude that democracy is readily put into practice, for the ICANN elections reveal numerous challenges that will have to be addressed in the future.

He further concluded that[19]

> most importantly, ICANN's global elections starkly manifested the value of democratic governance. The election served as a vehicle

for a reform movement. Democracy is more than a means to legitimacy: it is a means to better governance. By opening control of ICANN to user representatives, interests could be balanced and the original board's trajectory checked. ICANN's elections showed that not only is democracy feasible, it is vitally important to ensure balanced governance in a globalizing world.

Klein was prematurely optimistic. The board saw the at-large election as too complex and unpredictable to be used in the future. They quickly moved to develop a new procedure for electing board members. They used the model that had been applied in the IETF, the NomCom (nominating committee) and eventually agreed on a procedure that would be less transparent but more efficient (and predictable). The NomCom would select eight members of the board of directors, of which three would come from a new Country Code Names Supporting Organization (ccNSO), three from a Generic Names Supporting Organization (GNSO) and five from an Interim At-Large Advisory Committee (ALAC). The NomCom itself would be composed of 23 persons drawn from the various constituencies including the Root Server System Advisory Committee (RSSAC), the Security and Stability Advisory Committee (SSAC) and the Governmental Advisory Committee (GAC); the ALAC; delegates representing small business users and large business users, the Registry Constituency, the Registrars Constituency, the ccNSO, the ISP Constituency, the IP Constituency, the Address Supporting Organization (ASO), an entity representing academic and similar organizations; the Non-Commercial Users Constituency, the IETF and the Technical Liaison Group (TLG). This large, if cumbersome body, would then elect the directors.[20]

While classical electoral democracy was not achieved, a somewhat open process has been followed. Equally as important, the non-governmental actors learned that organizing was a means to influence outcomes. At subsequent meetings on Internet governance in ICANN as well as other forums, civil society has established the practice of creating civil society statements and these have begun to carry some weight in the debates.

ICANN structure

The current ICANN structure reflects the evolution from the early period. In 2002, under the second CEO, Stuart Lynn (also an academic who had been chief information officer of the University of California System), who had replaced Michael Roberts in 2001, a Committee on Restructuring was established. According to ICANN, the committee, subsequently renamed Committee on ICANN Evolution and Reform, was established "in view of considerable discussion at that time within the ICANN community of possible changes in the structure of ICANN, including possible new Supporting Organizations and new or revised mechanisms for selecting ICANN Directors." This reflected the problems with GDSO and the at-large election, and the fact that different groups of stakeholders were unhappy about their participation.

The committee worked during 2002 and, at the October meeting in Shanghai its recommendations were adopted by the board in the form of revised by-laws. The reform process was remarkably open, and most of the concerned groups of stakeholders made an input. The reform was in that sense the kind of rough consensus that had become the primary means of decision-making. The revision also corresponded to the search for a new CEO. The reform led to the current structure, which, in addition to maintaining the original Address Supporting Organization, converted the unwieldy DNSO into two different organizations, one dealing with generic names (for example .com, .org, .edu, .net) and another to deal with the emerging country-code names. It converted the Protocol Supporting Organization into three advisory groups and committees dealing with broad technical liaison with IETF, with the root server system and with security and stability. To deal with "other" input, it created an At-Large Advisory Committee that could provide a vehicle for users of the system to make an input. It maintained the Governmental Advisory Committee that had always existed, but made it much more important, as will be seen below.

In picking the new CEO, the ICANN board chose someone from a different epistemic community. Unlike his predecessors, Paul Twomey was not from academia or the technical community. Instead his experience was with government and business. He had been in the Australian government and, in fact, had chaired the Governmental Advisory Committee. In the Australian government he had been CEO of the National Office for the Information Economy and before that had been in the private sector with the Australian Trade Commission. This was related to a change in focus for ICANN from purely technical matters of root server administration into wider areas of policy.

The complex structure that emerged from the reorganization provides a place for the main interest groups. Figure 6.2 shows the structure as of 2007.

The central decision-making body is the board of directors. As noted, eight of the board members are now elected at-large through the NomCom process. The remaining board members come from supporting organizations, which also use a NomCom process. This means that

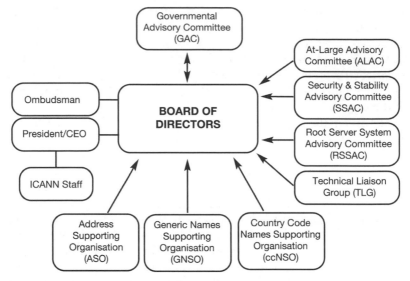

Figure 6.2 Structure of ICANN, October 2007.
Source: www.icann.org, structure, 27 October 2007.

anyone can nominate themselves, but the finalists will reflect a consensus among the presumably neutral or at least balanced committees.
In addition, liaisons elected by the advisory committees sit on the
board as non-voting members. By being open, the process should lead
to a board that reflects the main stakeholders.

To a large extent, this has been achieved. Table 6.2 shows the composition of the board in October 2007. Of the 21 members, 16 with the
right to vote, 5 are women, 14 are not from the United States. Most are
from the private sector, but there are at least four who represent what
could be called the non-governmental and academic communities. The
private sector members come from the computer industry, telecommunications and intellectual property. The only stakeholder that is
not strongly represented is government, since the only official on the
board is the liaison with the Government Advisory Committee,
Ambassador Janis Karklins. However, a number of the members had
previous experience with the United Nations in different capacities.

Creating a sense of legitimacy, the president of the board was, until
the final board meeting of 2007, Vint Cerf, whose most recent position
was as guru for Google, Inc., one of the most dynamic private sector
companies based on the Internet. He voluntarily left the position and
was replaced, on the basis of a contested vote at the October 2007

Table 6.2 Members of the ICANN board of directors, October 2007

Member	Nationality	Current position	Sex	International experience	Representing	Voting
Raimundo Beca	Chile	Imaginacción, a Chilean consulting company; previously Chile Teleccm	M	ECLAC Expert for 2 years	ASO Address Council	Yes
Vittorio Bertola	Italy	Freelance consultant in policy and technical projects	M	Business and NGO	At-large Advisory Committee	No
Vint Cerf	U.S.A.	Vice-President of Google	M	Founder of Internet		Yes
Susan P. Crawford	U.S.A.	Associate Professor of Law at Cardozo Law School	F	NGO activist		Yes
Stephen D. Crocker	U.S.A.	CEO and co-founder of Shinkuro, Inc	M	Founder of Internet	Security and Stability Advisory Committee	No
Francisco da Silva	Portugal	Senior Councilor at Portugal Telecom Corporate Headquarters	M	European telecom networks	Technical Liaison Group	No
Peter Dengate Thrush	New Zealand	Intellectual property lawyer	M	ccTLD registries	Country Code Names Supporting Organization	Yes
Roberto Gaetano	Italy	IAEA software developer	M	European Telecommunication Standards Institute		Yes

Table continued on next page.

Table 6.2 (continued)

Member	Nationality	Current position	Sex	International experience	Representing	Voting
Demi Getschko	Brazil	Brazilian Internet Steering Committee	M		Country Code Names Supporting Organization	Yes
Steve Goldstein	U.S.A.	Retired from National Science Foundation	M	International academic networks		Yes
Janis Karklins	Latvia	Ambassador to UN in Geneva	M	WSIS	Governmental advisory committee	Yes
Thomas Narten	U.S.A.	IBM software developer	M	IETF	IETF liaison	No
Rajasekhar Ramaraj	India	CEO of Sify Limited, the pioneer and leader in Internet, networking and e-commerce services in India	M			Yes
Joichi Ito	Japan	Vice President of International and Mobility Development for Technorati, which indexes and monitors blogs; and Chairman of Six Apart, the weblog software company	M	NGO activist		Yes
Njeri Rionge	Kenya	CEO and founder, Ignite Consulting and Investment Limited, and Director and co-founder, Wananchi Online Limited	F	International business		Yes

Table 6.2 (continued)

Member	Nationality	Current position	Sex	International experience	Representing	Voting
Rita Rodin	U.S.A.	Partner in Skadden's intellectual property and technology and Internet and e-commerce practices	F	Work on ICANN standards	Generic Names Supporting Organization	Yes
Vanda Scartezini	Brazil	She is the co-founder of and has been an active partner in Polo Consultores, a Brazilian IT consulting company	F	Was a Brazilian government official		Yes
Bruce Tonkin	Australia	Chief Technology Officer for Melbourne IT Limited	M	Registrar's constituency	Generic Names Supporting Organization	Yes
Paul Twomey	Australia	CEO of ICANN	M	Australian government and business		Yes
David L. Wodelet	Canada	Director of Internet Systems Engineering for Shaw Communications	M	Registrars	Address Supporting Organization	Yes
Suzanne Woolf	U.S.A.	Software engineer for Internet Systems Consortium, Inc	F	Worked with ICANN since 2002	Root Server System Advisory Committee	No

board meeting, by Peter Dengate-Thrush, from New Zealand, who was supported by the NGOs on the board.

The stakeholders and their role

As it has evolved under the leadership of Paul Twomey, ICANN has consciously sought to ensure representation by the various stakeholders. The effectiveness of their representation has had some consequences for the way in which ICANN has functioned, as will be shown.

Governments

The main stakeholder with a limited involvement in ICANN has been governments. The original motivation for establishing the institution was to remove management of what are now called critical Internet resources from government control. The comments on the White Paper showed that governments and international organizations were interested in ICANN and as a result the original ICANN by-laws made provision for a Governmental Advisory Committee to[21]

> consider and provide advice on the activities of ICANN as they relate to concerns of governments, multinational governmental organisations and treaty organisations, and distinct economies as recognised in international fora, including matters where there may be an interaction between ICANN's policies and various laws and international agreements and public policy objectives.

Membership was open to any government or international organization that was interested. Initially most of the members were from Europe but as interest in Internet governance has grown in developing countries, the composition of the GAC has changed. Table 6.3, drawn from a report of the GAC Chair to the Working Group on Internet Governance (see Chapter 7), shows the growth. In many respects, the GAC composition has begun to mirror that of the United Nations itself, with one key exception.

An initial concern of ICANN was with country-code top-level domain names. These are two-letter names that can designate countries. They include domains such as .us and .uk. The original intention was to allow countries to use their names to register sites. The United States, for example, originally used the .us name to register secondary schools (since universities had the .edu domain name) and later expanded it to include sub-national government sites. In the early, innocent days of the Internet, Jon Postel and his colleagues determined to use the ISO two-letter designation of countries. Many of the country-code names were not sovereign governments. In doing so, they made two political errors. First, the list was not politically correct since it included, in addition to China (.cn) and Hong Kong (.hk), Taiwan Province of China (.tw). Since the status of Taiwan (especially whether it could be considered independent) has yet to be resolved internationally, once ICANN took over the IANA functions, this had the effect of allowing Taiwan to participate in ICANN. And Taiwan does participate in GAC meetings, as did China, one of the few places where both would be represented. The GAC by-laws allow for this by permitting membership of "distinct economies as recognised in international fora." This avoids a judgment about the status of Taiwan.

Second, when IANA set up the country-level codes there was no procedure for determining, on the basis of governmental authority, who was qualified to provide registry services for the domain. Some of the two-letter domains had a value because of their meaning in English. For example, .tv (Tuvalu) could be used by television programs, .md (Moldova) could be used by medical sites and .fm (Federation of Micronesia) could be used by radio stations. Many countries did not have national registries so private individuals were given the authority to allocate domain names to some country-code domains.

When country codes became economically important, in addition to national pride, the GAC began to take an interest in how they were

Table 6.3 Composition of the Governmental Advisory Committee, by region, 1999–2004

Year	1999	2000	2001	2002	2003	2004
Africa	2	3	3	7	13	17
Middle East and North Africa	3	4	4	5	6	8
Asia-Pacific	14	18	19	19	21	24
Europe	23	26	30	30	31	37
Latin America and the Caribbean	5	7	9	10	11	11
North America	2	2	2	2	2	2
Members	49	60	67	73	84	99
Observers	5	5	5	6	6	9
Total	54	65	72	79	90	108

Source: ICANN, GAC chairman's report for the information of the United Nations Working Group on Internet Governance (WGIG) Geneva, February 2005.

allocated and managed. This also had to do with the basis under which country-code domain registrars would contribute to the ICANN budget.

Additionally, the GAC has become a kind of liaison between inter-governmental processes and ICANN and its influence has correspondingly increased.

Private sector

ICANN was set up essentially to represent the private sector. The Supporting Organizations are heavily dominated by representatives of private corporations. The address registries are among the most important since they are the link between ICANN and the Internet service providers. Similarly, the intellectual property establishment is well represented, having determined that domain names were critical property in an expanding Internet economy. In that sense, ICANN has been a good venue for that stakeholder, much better than, as we shall see, the intergovernmental forums.

Netizens

An early problem faced by ICANN was its relationship with users of the Internet, the so-called netizens. The first at-large election showed the extent of interest and influence of the user groups, who were initially loosely organized in the non-commercial domain holders group. Subsequently, civil society groups tended to work through the Generic Names Supporting Organization (GNSO). The GNSO was expected to represent the views of users and provide a bottom-up approach to policy. Like its predecessor, the DNSO, the GNSO is made up of six constituencies, the gTLD Registries (representing all gTLD registries under contract to ICANN), the Registrars (representing all registrars accredited by and under contract to ICANN), the Internet Service and Connectivity Providers (representing all entities providing Internet service and connectivity to Internet users), the Commercial and Business Users (representing both large and small commercial entity users of the Internet), the Intellectual Property Interests (representing the full range of trademark and other intellectual property interests relating to the DNS), and finally, the Non-Commercial Users (representing the full range of non-commercial entity users of the Internet).

Five of these really represent different private sector groups. Only the sixth, the non-commercial users, represented the more traditional civil society groups.

Each constituency elects three members of the GNSO council, which makes decisions that are passed on to the ICANN board, as well as electing the two board members provided by the GNSO. The process is multi-stage. Each of the constituencies has its own organization. Its members then participate in the GNSO in the open meetings directly and in the decision-making through their elected council members.

The Non-Commercial Users Constituency (NCUC) was made up of, as of 2006, 44 organizations from all of the regions. It includes organizations like the Association for Progressive Communications, the American Civil Liberties Union, Computer Professionals for Social Responsibility, and the Electronic Privacy Network. According to its by-laws,[22] the NCUC intends to represent the views and interests of those who engage in non-commercial speech and activity on the Internet and provide a voice and representation in ICANN processes to non-profit organizations that serve non-commercial interests and provide services such as education, community organizing, promotion of the arts, public interest policy advocacy, children's welfare, religion, scientific research, human rights, and the advancement of the Internet as a global communications system for all segments of society.

Like other stakeholder groups, the NCUC seeks balance in its governance structures. The current chair is Milton Mueller of the Internet Governance Project and Syracuse University. Mueller is an academic who has been involved with Internet governance and ICANN since the beginning. The GNSO council representatives included Robin Gross from the United States, who is the head of an NGO dealing with intellectual property, Norbert Klein from Cambodia representing the Open Institute of that country, and Mawaki Chango from Togo, representing the African Civil Society for the Information Society. Other members of the Executive Committee included:

- North America region: Robert Guerra, CPSR, Canada
- Europe region: Georg Grève, Free Software Foundation Europe, Germany
- Africa region: Olivier Nana Nzepa. Africa Management, Cameroun
- Latin America/Caribbean region: Marcelo Fernandes, The Committee for Democratization in Information Technology of Pernambuco, Brazil
- Asia-Pacific region: Horacio Cadiz, Philippine Network Foundation, The Philippines.

Many of the participants in the GNSO have been active also in the wider Internet governance machineries described in Chapters 7 and 8.

Petty administration or politics?

At one level, ICANN is a narrow technical body, an extension of the technical groups represented by the IETF, with which it maintains close ties. If this were its only function, presumably it would have done its management of the critical Internet resources in relative obscurity, as is often the case with technical bodies at the international level.

Because of the political and economic consequences of the information revolution built around the Internet, ICANN has had to become involved in policy issues to an extent that the White Paper did not envisage. The byplay of different stakeholders can be seen in three of the issues: how to deal with the country-code domain names; what to do with WHOIS; and the controversy about creating a top-level domain name for the adult content industry (.xxx).

Country-code domain names (cc-tlds)

The country-code issue involved both the private sector and governments. It involved a trade-off between the need to maintain an internationally open root system and the desire to protect national space. The issue was fought out over three distinct but related problems: how much to charge cc-tld registrars for belonging to ICANN, how to determine who should be a registrar, and whether multilingualism would be possible in domain names.

In one sense, country codes could be used to exclude domains from the Internet. If they are not registered in the central root server, they could communicate among themselves but not with the rest of the world. The registrars of the domains would be outside the influence of the central bodies. As a result, country-code registrars are not as dependent on ICANN as those registering generic top-level names. For this reason, ICANN has had to work to maintain the cc-tld registries within the ICANN system.

WHOIS and privacy

A long-term feature of the ICANN system has been the WHOIS database. Dating back to the early days of the Internet, each domain registrant was required to specify both a technical and an administrative contact in a searchable database.[23] WHOIS services provide public access to data on registered domain names, which currently includes contact information for Registered Name Holders. The extent of registration data collected at the time of registration of a domain name, and the ways such data can be accessed, are specified in agreements established by ICANN for domain names registered in generic top-level domains (gTLDs). For example, ICANN requires accredited registrars to collect and provide free public access to the name of the registered domain name and its nameservers and registrar, the date the domain was created and when its registration expires, and the contact information for the Registered Name Holder, the technical contact, and the administrative contact.

However, over time, it has become a vehicle for law enforcement authorities, as well as intellectual property lawyers, to identify the source of content. This led to concerns about privacy and, over a number of years, there have been efforts to reform the WHOIS database in order to address the issue. The responsibility for developing policy has been given to the GNSO, and its deliberations show some of the difficulties of maintaining multi-stakeholder governance.[24]

In June, 2005, the GNSO council convened a WHOIS Task Force to address a number of important questions related to WHOIS, including the purpose of WHOIS service, which information should be available to the public, how to improve WHOIS accuracy and how to deal with conflicts between WHOIS requirements and relevant privacy laws. The Task Force eventually produced a report in March 2007, but this was not a consensus document. The majority on the Task Force proposed replacing the current entries with a single Operative Point of Contact (OPOC). The majority included the Registry, Registrar and Non-Commercial User constituencies but not the Business Constituency, which issued a minority report. The latter group called for deferring action and conducting additional studies. This was seen by the other constituencies as an effort to postpone consideration. The matter was taken up at the GNSO meeting on 31 October 2007, where by a 10–13 vote, the matter was postponed.

The 10 votes in favor of the OPOC proposal came from the registries that had a majority on the working group, and included the GNSO chair, Avri Doria, an NGO advocate. The 13 against came from the three business-based constituencies.

The .xxx problem

A key ICANN function has been to authorize new generic top-level domain names. This was intended primarily to reduce the scarcity of .com domain names by adding others that would also clearly indicate the purpose of the domain. One of the early successes of ICANN has been to agree on 20 tlds, including 13 new ones, shown in Box 6.1.[25]

Box 6.1   Generic top-level domain names in force in October 2007

- The **.aero** domain is reserved for members of the air-transport industry and is sponsored by **Société Internationale de Télécommunications Aéronautiques (SITA)**.
- The **.asia** domain is restricted to the Pan-Asia and Asia-Pacific community and is operated by **DotAsia Organisation**.
- The **.biz** domain is restricted to businesses and is operated by **NeuLevel, Inc.**
- The **.cat** domain is reserved for the Catalan linguistic and cultural community and is sponsored by **Fundació puntCat**.
- The **.com** domain is operated by **VeriSign Global Registry Services**.
- The **.coop** domain is reserved for cooperative associations and is sponsored by **Dot Cooperation LLC**.
- The **.info** domain is operated by **Afilias Limited**.
- The **.jobs** domain is reserved for human resource managers and is sponsored by **Employ Media LLC**.
- The **.mobi** domain is reserved for consumers and providers of mobile products and services and is sponsored by **mTLD Top Level Domain, Ltd**.
- The **.museum** domain is reserved for museums and is sponsored by the **Museum Domain Management Association**.
- The **.name** domain is reserved for individuals and is operated by **Global Name Registry**.
- The **.net** domain is operated by **VeriSign Global Registry Services**.
- The **.org** domain is operated by **Public Interest Registry**. It is intended to serve the non-commercial community, but all are eligible to register within.org.
- The **.pro** domain is restricted to credentialed professionals and related entities and is operated by **RegistryPro**.
- The **.tel** domain is reserved for businesses and individuals to publish their contact data and is sponsored by **Telnic Ltd.**
- The **.travel** domain is reserved for entities whose primary area of activity is in the travel industry and is sponsored by **Tralliance Corporation**.

- The **.gov** domain is reserved exclusively for the United States government. It is operated by the **U.S. General Services Administration**.
- The **.edu** domain is reserved for post-secondary institutions accredited by an agency on the U.S. Department of Education's list of Nationally Recognized Accrediting Agencies and is registered only through **Educause**.
- The **.mil** domain is reserved exclusively for the United States military. It is operated by the **U.S. DoD Network Information Center**.
- The **.int** domain is used only for registering organizations established by international treaties between governments. It is operated by the **IANA.int Domain Registry**.

While the designation of new domain names was always somewhat contentious, the first major problem that became controversial was when the Internet Content Management (ICM) Registry in 2000 proposed creating a top-level domain .xxx for providers of adult content. In many countries, adult films were given an "x" rating, which was the basis for the domain name. This was immediately controversial, in part because what was considered adult content varied from country to country, in part because in some jurisdictions all adult content was considered pornographic or obscene, and in part because of child pornography, which was globally prohibited under international conventions as noted in Chapter 5.

The application tested the ICANN process. Like all applications, the .xxx application was subject to comments from different stakeholders. There were many comments, but the Government Advisory Committee (GAC) showed an unusual interest. After a prolonged negotiation with ICM, the ICANN board in June 2005 authorized its staff to enter into negotiations about the .xxx domain name. As was customary, the proposal was sent out for comment. Conservatives with connections to the United States government mounted a campaign against the proposal, and several other governments showed concern. The proposal was taken up by the GAC in its March 2006 meeting in New Zealand, and the consensus was that the proposal was flawed, but added that "several members of the GAC are emphatically opposed from a public policy perspective to the introduction of a .xxx sTLD."[26]

Faced with the opposition, the board voted in May 2006 not to approve the application, but sent it back for retooling. The vote was five in favor to nine against. The GAC position produced a two-fold reaction. The European Union expressed concern that the United States government was compromising the independence of ICANN. This was echoed by the *New York Times* which editorialized that "the department's [the U.S. Department of Commerce] behavior looks a lot like political pressure. That sends the wrong message to moderates in Europe on the issue of Internet control. The United States should not give even the appearance of improper lobbying. If Americans cannot trust the system to run itself, they risk losing it."[27]

Non-governmental organizations also took issue with the decision. Milton Mueller noted in an article published by the Internet Governance Project, that the controversy was giving ICANN a policy role that it was not equipped to undertake.[28] The decision would establish a role for a body that was essentially unaccountable to censor content on the Internet or allow others to do so.

The proposal was re-submitted, but on 30 March 2007, the ICANN board voted nine to five against accepting the proposal, effectively killing it. In terms of geography there was no pattern in the vote, but most of those representing civil society voted to allow the proposal to advance.

The U.S. control issue: who should control the critical Internet resources

The .xxx controversy highlighted a growing concern with control of ICANN and through it of the Internet by the United States government. The assumption made in the White Paper in 1998 was that the U.S. government would gradually phase out its involvement so that ICANN would become a self-standing private body. The .xxx issue showed that domestic politics still had a hand. More importantly, the policies of the Bush administration, emphasizing unilateral action, including its involvement in Iraq, had led to a growing consensus that the Internet needed to be freed from unilateral governmental control.

ICANN itself has sought to blunt the issue by renegotiating its contract with the United States Department of Commerce to provide addressing services. The most recent contract is dated 11 August 2006 and is for five years. At the same time, the arrangement has increasingly been questioned, by both other governments and by non-governmental organizations. This emerged visibly at the World Summit on the Information Society, to which we must now turn.

7 Multi-stakeholderism emerges from the World Summit on the Information Society

The Internet grew dramatically, as did its problems, and ICANN began to expand, but the international political dimension of Internet governance did not emerge until the World Summit on the Information Society in 2003. This led to a reflection on what kinds of institutions and arrangement might be needed, and solidified a growing approach based on effectively involving all stakeholders in governance, a new model for international institutions.

While the management of the critical Internet resources was being developed through ICANN, the intergovernmental system was also becoming interested in Internet governance. The International Telecommunications Union (ITU) secretariat had sought to become involved through the MoU-TLD and had almost succeeded when opposition in the United States had derailed the project in 1997. At the same time that the White Paper was being considered, the ITU was holding its quadrennial Plenipotentiary Conference in Minneapolis, Minnesota. The ITU was trying to adapt to rapidly changing information technology that had made much of what it had been doing obsolete. This coincided with an increased interest in other United Nations organs with the role of information and communication technologies in development. One of the recommendations from Minneapolis was that a World Summit on the Information Society (WSIS) be convened. Organizing a world conference or summit has been a favorite vehicle for launching new or revised international initiatives to solve global problems, as has been analyzed by Michael Schechter in another volume in this series.[1]

Finding an identity: origins of WSIS

ITU's governments meet every four years to discuss policies for the organization. This usually involves approving a plan for the next four years, electing or re-electing the director-general and dealing with technical policy issues. In 1998, the future identity of ITU was very much in question. As the backgrounder prepared for the session, held from 12 October to 6 November 1998, put it:[2]

> As the world stands on the brink, not only of the next millennium but of a powerful new age of information and communications capabilities, the world's pre-eminent telecommunications organiza- tion also finds itself at a crossroads. As it prepares to convene for its fifteenth Plenipotentiary Conference in just a few weeks, the challenge facing the ITU is stark and simple: re-adapt quickly to a rapidly changing telecommunications environment, or find itself marginalized or at worst irrelevant in the future development of the world's communications networks.

The main concerns were the fact that telecommunications deregulation had changed the nature of stakeholders in the ITU. Globalization was increasing the transnational aspects of telecommunications. Telecom companies that had formerly been run by governments were becoming privatized. "Convergence between the telecommunications, information technology and audiovisual entertainment industries is blurring the distinction between formerly disparate technologies and equipment." In short, there was a need for reform.

At the very end of the backgrounder, almost as an afterthought, the ITU observed that the Internet would need attention because of the organization's work with standards and standard-setting organizations like the IETF. It noted the failed MoUtld and noted that "the US has since come up with its own proposal, which has raised concerns in both political circles and in the Internet community at large. Any fur- ther ITU involvement in the management and governance of the Internet and other new communications systems is therefore certain to be a hot topic in Minneapolis."[3]

The conference was unable to reach an agreement on what to do. At the suggestion of the president of Tunisia, Ben Ali, who focused on ICT for development and the need to enhance it, the conference adopted a resolution that instructed the ITU director-general to "place the question of the holding of a World Summit on the Information Society (WSIS) on the agenda of the the United Nations System Chief Executive Board—CEB—and to report to the ITU governing body, the Council, on the results of that consultation."[4] The need to deal with the UN system as a whole was a recognition that ITU lacked a mandate to cover all of the relevant issues.

The newly elected director-general, Yoshio Utsumi, who had been a telecommunications official with the Japanese government, proceeded to raise the question in the CEB, which is composed of the executive heads of all United Nations system organizations. According to the ITU, the CEB reacted positively and a majority of other organizations and agencies had expressed interest in being associated with the preparation and holding of the summit.[5] According to the ITU, this was reported to the ITU council and "It was decided that the Summit would be held under the high patronage of the UN Secretary-General, with ITU taking the lead role in preparations." This meant that the United Nations Secretariat would be involved in the preparations.

The United Nations was already becoming engaged with information and communications technology. The Economic and Social Council (ECOSOC), at the initiative both of the UN Secretariat who saw this as an issue that needed discussion, and a number of delegations from developing countries, decided to take up the issue at its high-level segment in 2000. ECOSOC organizes its work around themes for which it expects ministerial-level participation and the 2000 session, held before the Millennium Summit, provided an opportunity for the United Nations to take a broad view of ICT. The formal title of the theme was "Development and International Cooperation in the Twenty-first Century: The Role of Information Technology in the Context of a Knowledge-based Global Economy."

The 2000 ECOSOC session was held in New York (the sessions alternate between New York and Geneva) and over two days, a series of panels and speeches took place. A large number of ministers spoke, as did the heads of several UN system bodies including the president of the World Bank, the director-general of WTO, the deputy managing director of IMF, and the secretary-general of the United Nations Conference on Trade and Development. The director-general of the ITU did not speak, although a lower-level representative did towards the end of the discussion. The private sector, in what was a major innovation for the United Nations, was given a prominent place. The ECOSOC report for the year noted that keynote addresses were also made by Wolfgang Kemna, chief executive officer, World Tel; John Gage, chief scientist, Sun Microsystems; and Vinton Cerf, senior vice-president of World Com and former president of the Internet Society.[6]

The selection, brokered by the UN Division for Economic and Social Council Support and Coordination, headed by Sarbuland Khan, a career official, reflected a careful balance between the telecommunications industry, the computer industry and the technical community represented by Cerf. In ECOSOC debates, non-governmental organizations are permitted to participate, on a limited basis. The NGOs who spoke included the International Chamber of Commerce, the Conference of Non-Governmental Organizations in consultative relationship with the United Nations (CONGO), Population Communication-International, World Information Transfer, and Women Action 2000 (on behalf of the Association tunisie 21).

The session adopted a ministerial declaration reflecting a consensus on ICT for development. It included references to issues such as the digital divide, development and transfer of new information technologies and increasing globalization. The only mention of the Internet, however, was in terms of developing local content and the ability of people to freely access it,[7] which

> will help foster a culturally and linguistically diverse cyberspace and encourage broad and sustainable use of the Internet. Local content can also facilitate entrance to the knowledge-based economy for individuals and firms in developing countries and also as a means to expand their participation in the new networked economy.

At the UN Millennium Summit in September that adopted the Millennium Development Goals, ICT was included under the goal of developing a global partnership for development. The goal stated "In cooperation with the private sector, make available the benefits of new technologies—especially information and communications technologies." While the focus was on technological transfer, it did include the idea that the private sector was a major stakeholder. This was part of a larger effort to incorporate the increasingly transnational private sector into governance discussions. The most comprehensive reflection was the Global Compact, a network of businesses and non-governmental organizations to support United Nations initiatives that was launched in July 2000, about the same time as the ECOSOC session.

ITU secretary-general Utsumi briefed the chief executives board on WSIS in October 2000 saying that the decision to convene WSIS had received a positive reaction from both the public and private sectors and proposed that the summit "be convened by the Secretary-General of the United Nations, and indicated that the anticipated outcome of the Summit would be a declaration of universal political will and a concrete action programme for achieving the goals of the information society."[8]

The CEB expressed its satisfaction with the draft plan of action and stressed the importance of an early decision by ITU on the venue of the summit.

Encouraged by the ECOSOC and the Millennium Summit, the next year (2001) the ITU council decided to set up the summit in two phases. The first would be in Geneva in November 2003 and the second in Tunis in November 2005. The dual location summit was prompted by the fact that both Tunisia and Switzerland had offered to host the summit. When multiple locations were offered in other cases, a conflict usually ensued, as happened with the Fourth World Conference on Women when both China and Austria offered (eventually China won, with Austria getting the World Conference on Human Rights as a consolation prize). In this case, Switzerland offered to provide considerable resources, while Tunisia argued that the summit should be in a developing country. The compromise was to have, in effect, two summits.

The ITU again briefed the chief executives board about the plans at the October 2001 session. He noted that the Geneva phase would be particularly important to bring together the views of non-governmental actors.

The General Assembly adopted a resolution authorizing the World Summit. The resolution was necessary for the United Nations Secretariat to be a part of the process. The resolution was introduced by Tunisia, with co-sponsorship by the Russian Federation and Mauritania under the General Assembly agenda item on science and technology for development. The third operative paragraph of the draft resolution tried to establish ITU's predominant role in WSIS. It read:

> 3. *Encourages* effective contributions from and the active participation of all relevant United Nations bodies, in particular the Information and Communication Technologies Task Force, and encourages other intergovernmental organizations, including international and regional institutions, non-governmental organizations, civil society and the private sector to cooperate actively with the Secretary-General of the International Telecommunication Union in preparing for the Summit.

The Information and Communication Technologies Task Force (ICT-D) had been set up as part of the follow-up to the ECOSOC discussion, was headed by the former president of Costa Rica, Jose Maria Figueres, and was a multi-stakeholder group including both governments and non-governmental actors, especially private corporations. It reflected the rivalry between the ITU and the other United Nations secretariats over the issue. For this reason, in the negotiations over the draft resolution, the only major change came to that paragraph. The finally agreed text gave a less decisive role to ITU, by inviting it "to assume the leading managerial role in the executive secretariat of the Summit and its preparatory process."

In other words, the ITU would do most of the work, but would not really be in charge. The final version also strengthened the role of non-governmental stakeholders in the process by modifying the original proposal to read:

> 5. *Encourages* effective contributions from and the active partici-
> pation of all relevant United Nations bodies, in particular the
> Information and Communication Technologies Task Force, and
> encourages other intergovernmental organizations, including inter-
> national and regional institutions, non-governmental organiza-
> tions, civil society and the private sector, to contribute to, and
> actively participate in, the intergovernmental preparatory process
> of the Summit and the Summit itself.

The General Assembly also acted to ensure that the preparation process was open, including provision for participation by the private sector and other non-governmental stakeholders. The resolution (56/183) recommended that "the preparation for the Summit take place through an open-ended intergovernmental preparatory committee, which would define the agenda of the Summit, finalize both the draft declaration and the draft plan of action, and decide on the modalities of the participation of other stakeholders in the Summit." The resolution did not mention the Internet at all, and it could be assumed that WSIS' main focus would be on information technology transfer.

WSIS I: Internet governance emerges

The key events for intergovernmental summits are the preparatory meetings. These are intended to solve most procedural and substantive issues and, under the best of circumstances, bring an almost agreed text to the final event so that either the final document can be approved without debate or the debates can be focused on a limited number of issues on which agreement had not been reached. The organizers of WSIS knew this and envisaged a relatively long preparatory process. Between the formal agreement to hold WSIS, reflected in the General Assembly resolution, and the first summit in December 2003, plans were made to hold three preparatory meetings. As these unfolded, starting in July 2002, the issues became clearer and the final outcome of the Geneva phase was determined.

The first meeting of the Preparatory Committee ran from 1–5 July 2002 in Geneva. It was largely prepared by the ITU. The inaugural session was considered informal because some of the speakers were not representatives of governments or international organizations. The initial speakers were chosen to represent the different stakeholder groups. In addition to the secretary-general of ITU, speakers included a representative from Switzerland and the ambassador of Tunisia (representing the host countries), the under-secretary-general for Public Information (representing the UN Secretariat), the secretary-general of the International Chamber of Commerce (representing the private sector) and the president of Fundación Redes y Desarrollo (Funredes) from the Dominican Republic (representing civil society). The fact that the senior UN representative was from public information means that the UN had not yet decided how it was supposed to participate in WSIS.

A major debate focused on the rules for permitting non-state actors to participate. This has always been contentious in international organizations, since governments do not want to grant access to organizations that might be hostile to them. The organizations interested in ICT tapped a constituency that was unique and the existing rules would not have permitted many of them to participate, particularly from the private sector.

On substantive issues, an initial consultation took place as a subcommittee of the PrepCom, but no formal outcome was determined. The chairman of the subcommittee, from Mexico, produced what is called in the UN a "non-paper" (meaning that it had no formal, official standing but could be used as a basis for discussion) that did not include governance issues. However, a compilation of statements made showed that non-governmental organizations had proposed: "The creation of an enabling regulatory and policy framework was also suggested as a possible theme."[9]

Since little progress had been made on the substance at the first PrepCom, so an informal meeting was called in Geneva from 16–18 September 2002. There was considerable participation by governments, international secretariats and NGOs, but mostly from those located in Geneva.

The method of work was to allow interested parties to make proposals that would then be considered for inclusion in the outcome document of the meeting. After the first day, the only reflection of the governance issue was a statement that "Global governance of the Information Society should be also considered." The issue, however, was raised in several contributions. For example, the International Atomic Energy Agency, usually not an important player in ICT, said, "We also note that significant parts of the Internet are controlled by a privately owned US company. The regulatory framework for the Internet needs to be defined by an international treaty and certain central functions need to be assigned to an international organisation (e.g. ITU)."

At the end of the consultation, a set of conclusions were presented. In the United Nations, to facilitate negotiation, texts that are not yet agreed are shown in square brackets ([ ]). The issue of an enabling environment was included, but clearly not agreed and with alternative formulations presented:[10]

> [[Enabling [a national and international] environment notably] [policies and regulatory frameworks][and establishing codes of conduct for business and enterprises]]

PrepCom 2

The second Preparatory Committee was scheduled to take place in Geneva from 17–28 February 2003. This was expected to be the major event to shape the summit's final document. It fulfilled its expectations. There were 1,600 individual participants representing 774 different entities. Table 7.1 shows the distribution of participants and entities. WSIS being a governmental conference, the largest proportion of participants represented governmental entities (called Administrations by the ITU). There were relatively few business representatives but a quarter were from non-governmental organizations. This was a pattern that would continue through Tunis.

The session started with what was called a "visionaries panel" and a series of thematic roundtables. None of these mentioned Internet governance as an issue, although Lawrence Lessig, one of the visionaries, emphasized the need for an open Internet. However, different participants had developed policy proposals in advance of the session. While most dealt with what were considered conventional ICT issues, several mentioned Internet governance as an issue. Specifically, Brazil stated, in its comment on themes and issues:

> Internet has evolved into a global public good and its governance should constitute a core issue of the Information Society agenda. Developing countries should have full access to and take part in all decision-making bodies and processes concerning the structure and functioning of the cyberspace, within which public, private and non-governmental agents will increasingly conduct their social and economic activities.

Table 7.1 Participants in Preparatory Committee 2, February 2003, by type

Type	Participants		Entities	
	Number	%	Number	%
Governments	909	58.6	484	62.5
Business	60	3.9	32	4.1
UN system	128	8.2	37	4.8
Other intergovernmental organizations	61	3.9	21	2.7
Non-governmental organizations	394	25.4	200	25.8
Total	1552	100.0	774	100.0

The many non-governmental organizations, knowing that individually they would not have much influence over the proceedings, decided to organize into what was called the Civil Society Coordination Group. This consisted of 37 organizations, including a number who had been active in ICANN, such as the Association for Progressive Communication and Computer Professionals for Social Responsibility. They prepared a joint statement in December 2002, negotiating the text over the Internet, an innovation in itself. The statement included a proposal to include the theme of Rights, Responsibilities, and Governance:[11]

> In this category, WSIS would address the rights of citizens and communities in the information society as well as the particulars of governing the Information Society. Themes would include: governance of information and communication societies in a globalised world, democratic management of international bodies dealing with ICTs, including Internet governance, with emphasis on developing and securing the global information commons and a right of universal access; democratic management of the Internet Domain Name and IP Address System, including the political as well as technical issues of the management process.

Along the same lines, the Latin American Regional Conference, held from 29–31 January 2003 in the Dominican Republic, included in its recommendations that

> The responsibility for root directories and domain names should rest with a suitable international organization and should take multilingualism into consideration. Countries' top-level-domain-names and Internet Protocol (IP) address assignment should be the

sovereign right of countries. The sovereignty of each nation should
be protected and respected. Internet governance should be multilateral, democratic and transparent and should take into account
the needs of the public and private sectors as well as those of the
civil society;

This proposal, made by governments, was included in the draft adopted at the end of the PrepCom, with the exception that an alternative
formulation to "international (inter-governmental)" was placed in the
text.[12]

In addition the draft Plan of Action as recommended by Subcommittee
2 included ideas from the Civil Society Coalition:[13] Multilateral,
transparent and democratic Internet governance should form part of
this effort, taking into account the needs of the public and private
sectors, as well as those of civil society.

Progress in agreeing on the text was sufficiently slow that another
informal meeting was agreed. Informal meetings are often preferred as
a way of obtaining text to negotiate. Because formal rules about
speaking, who can make suggestions and how texts are assembled are
not followed, the informals allow a more open exchange and non-state
actors can play a role. The Bureau of WSIS decided to authorize a
formal open-ended intergovernmental drafting group that would meet
intersessionally to improve the draft text. The bureau of any intergovernmental body consists of the office-bearers (chairs, vice-chairs
and rapporteurs) elected by the body and reflecting strict geographical
distribution. It holds procedural discussions. It is normally restricted to
governments, and non-state actors have often been concerned with
being excluded. Moreover, WSIS was running under UN rules that
made procedural innovations difficult.

Informal intersession

The informal intersession took place from 15–18 July 2003 in Paris.
The starting points of the discussions were supposed to be a draft
Declaration of Principles and a draft Plan of Action that the chairman
and the WSIS secretariat compiled from the February discussions.
Their first version, issued in March, received extensive comments and a
new version was issued on 5 June 2003. Following the custom in international organizations, comments on specific paragraphs of the drafts
were issued. They suggested the outlines of conflicts over Internet
governance. While there was general acceptance of the notion that
Internet governance should be multilateral, democratic and transparent,

there was no consensus about critical Internet resources, including management of the root server system. There seemed to be a consensus among the governments who commented that the coordination responsibility for root servers, domain names, and Internet Protocol (IP) address assignment should rest with a suitable international, intergovernmental organization. However, even among non-governmental organizations this was not a consensus position. The APC, for example, expressed satisfaction with ICANN, although cautioning against letting it expand into the policy arena. The Internet Society defended ICANN as did GLOCOM, the Japanese Institute of Global Communications that represented both academic and business interests.

Reflecting the increased need to give non-state actors a place in the discussions, the Bureau of the PrepCom made provision for observers to speak both at the beginning of the session and at a mid-point. On this basis 12 intergovernmental organizations spoke, as did 16 NGOs and nine private sector representatives. These numbers included individuals who were key players in the subsequent process. For example, one of the NGOs was the University of Aarhus, but this was in fact Wolfgang Kleinwächter, a professor from Germany with a specific interest in Internet governance. The speaker for the International Chamber of Commerce was Aleysha Hassan, an official whose main concern was the Internet and who was able to speak authoritatively for the business community.

The consultation divided its work among four smaller groups, dealing with Right to Communicate, Internet Management, Good Governance, and Network Security. These were all Internet issues. Internet management referred to a paragraph describing, among other things, the ICANN function, which was considered controversial because there was a difference of opinion between governments, business and civil society.

Over the informals, changes were made in the text, expanding and dividing some of the concepts so that they could be negotiated separately. One basis for changes is formal submissions in advance by participants. These submissions marked limits that governments set for consensus, as well as providing civil society with an opportunity to put ideas on the table. In the Paris consultations the United States was very clear that it defended the WTO and WIPO approaches to intellectual property and considered that the management of the root servers should not be taken up at all. Specifically, its comment stated: "the management of the Internet domain name and address system should take place via a public-private partnership that operates in an open and transparent manner to preserve and enhance the necessary global interoperability and coordination of the Internet's unique identifier system while recognizing its technical limitations and requirements."

The consultations identified a set of conflicts that needed to be resolved. First, while there was a consensus that Internet governance should be multilateral and transparent, there was no consensus about whether it should be a multi-stakeholder as contrasted with a government-driven process. Second, the nature of Internet governance was not defined.

PrepCom 3

The final preparatory committee was expected to take place from 15–26 September 2003 so that the Declaration and Plan of Action could be agreed well in advance of the summit. It was assumed that the informal intersessional meeting would have narrowed the areas of disagreement sufficiently that consensus on the text could be reached. This was not the case. In fact, the third PrepCom had to meet again in November and then again in December just before the summit to reach agreement.

This is not unusual in international meetings where new subjects are on the table about which there are no pre-existing agreements. This was particularly the case with the Internet. Agreement on some of the usual issues of ICT for Development was relatively easy, since there had been some pre-existing text coming from other forums. Some issues, like financing of development, would not be resolved because there were disagreements more broadly and these could not be resolved in what was considered a technical conference.

The Internet, however, had not been dealt with anywhere else and the preliminary discussions had revealed that it was qualitatively different from other communications systems for which there were existing institutions like the ITU. Achieving an understanding about what Internet governance means lacked any pre-existing "agreed text." The discussions in PrepCom 2 and the Intersession Informals had clearly indicated the areas of disagreement.

Governments had begun to see how the Internet raised policy issues and civil society had begun to press their concerns. The private sector, although it had been invited, played primarily a blocking role, seeking to ensure that text was not adopted that constrained the private sector. The PrepCom process also involved a debate over how non-state actors could be involved in the negotiations.

The fact that WSIS was now a United Nations conference meant that United Nations rules would apply. These had evolved over time to give a much more active role to non-state actors. The United Nations women's conferences (Mexico City in 1975, Copenhagen in 1980,

Nairobi in 1985 and Beijing in 1995) had had active NGO participation, as had the 1992 Rio conference on the environment. There had been major disputes about accreditation that had been resolved in favor of almost universal accreditation of interested groups, provided that they were not objectionable to a member state on political grounds. There was less agreement on the extent to which non-state actors could participate in negotiations, which were assumed to be a matter of governments. Most NGOs in those conferences learned that they could make their opinions heard either in the preparatory processes, which were more open and informal than final conventions, or by influencing national delegations to take up their positions. Some NGOs made an effort to place active members on national delegations.

At this point, the United Nations Secretariat decided to take a major role, eclipsing in many ways that of the ITU. Secretary-General Kofi Annan appointed Nitin Desai from India as his Special Representative to WSIS on 23 July 2003. Desai had been the under-secretary-general for Economic and Social Affairs until he retired in 2002. He had been one of the executives at the Rio environmental conference and the 2002 follow-up conference in Johannesburg, and had credibility with both governments and the NGO community. Moreover, he was interested in and knowledgeable about ICT. Coming right after the conclusion of the Paris informals, his appointment reflected a sense that the negotiations on the draft declaration and plan of action were not going well.

Between the Paris informals and the scheduled start of PrepCom 3, the secretariat prepared a new consolidated draft of the Declaration and the Plan of Action that reflected the Paris discussions. The text had a very large amount of bracketed (not agreed) text, including all of that relating to Internet governance. The bracketed text was the starting point for the consultations.

The PrepCom was very well attended. Table 7.2 shows the participation by type of entity. As can be seen, the number of participants, compared with PrepCom 2 increased by 100, almost completely explained by increased participation of non-governmental organizations.

The complexity of the negotiation process led to the creation of subcommittees and working groups to deal with specific texts. Again, non-governmental organizations and the private sector were given a chance to speak, putting text ideas on the table for discussion. In response to pressure from the NGOs, the Bureau decided that "It was agreed that observers could attend the discussions in the Plenary and Working Group Meetings and would be invited by the Chairperson to make brief statements. Observers were also invited to make brief statements at the start of each ad hoc group meeting." While not

Table 7.2 Participants in Preparatory Committee 3, September 2003, by type

Type	Participants		Entities	
	Number	%	Number	%
Governments	887	53.5	481	60.0
Business	68	4.1	33	4.1
UN system	97	5.9	33	4.1
Other intergovernmental organizations	68	4.1	4	0.5
Non-governmental organizations	537	32.4	250	31.2
Total	1657	100.0	801	100.0

unprecedented, this concession gave non-state actors access to the negotiations on a scale that was not at all usual.

In the discussions of the Internet management issue, one concept that had been championed by the civil society caucus was that information on the Internet was a public good. If so, it was subject to public oversight rather than merely the operations of the market. In the first revised draft of the Declaration this concept was placed into the discussion. The relevant paragraph read:

> 39. [44.] The Internet has evolved into a global public [good]/ [infrastructure]/[resource] and its governance should constitute a core issue of the Information Society agenda. The international management of the Internet should be multilateral, transparent and democratic, with the full involvement of governments, the private sector, civil society and international organizations. It should ensure an equitable distribution of resources, facilitate access for all and ensure a stable and secure functioning of the Internet, taking into account multilingualism.

By the end of the negotiations, however, the term "public good" had been eliminated from the draft, presumably because of the implications for regulation. However, the concept that management of the Internet was more than a technical matter had also been injected into the text. In doing so, the private sector interest was also included, with different views on whether this interest was merely technical or went beyond it. The draft read:

> 40. The management of the Internet encompasses both technical and policy issues. The private sector has had and will continue to have an important role in the development of the Internet [at the

technical level]. [Alternative 40. The management of the Internet encompasses both technical and public policy issues. The private sector has had an important role in the development of the Internet. The private sector should continue to play an important role at the technical and commercial levels.]

The issue was rejoined at the renewed meeting of PrepCom 3 in Geneva from 10–14 November. In between the two meetings, informal consultations were held. The November meeting was difficult. Its starting point was a non paper prepared by the president of the PrepCom (with the help of the secretariat). In that paper, the Internet governance part was still in brackets but the public good/infrastructure/resource reference had been converted to what would become the final text: "The Internet has evolved into a global facility available to the public and its governance should constitute a core issue of the Information Society agenda." This was clearly a compromise pushed by governments and the private sector who would not want a statement that the Internet was inherently public and therefore subject to regulation. The non-paper showed that other parts of the draft were not agreed either.

The report of the final phase of PrepCom 3 stated that "on some substantial issues, like human rights, Internet governance, role of the media, network security and financing, the consensus on a common text was still outstanding."[14] These were all sections on which civil society, the private sector and governments had different views, and all were related to the Internet. The issue of human rights, for example, was the extent to which—and how—international human rights applied to the Internet. This carried over to issues of intellectual property.

The final negotiation process, which carried on until the eve of WSIS itself, was restricted to governments. Different facilitators were charged with finding solutions to the unagreed text. The last issue to be resolved was Internet governance. Like all consensus agreements, the solution was based first on a clearer (and longer) text describing the roles of different stakeholders in governance. The second element was to pass the disputes on to a new body, therefore delaying the necessity of the decision.

The main implication of the text of the Declaration that was finally agreed and which WSIS adopted at the Geneva part of the summit was:

> to ask the Secretary-General of the United Nations to set up a working group on Internet governance, in an open and inclusive process that ensures a mechanism for the full and active participation of governments, the private sector and civil society from both developing and developed countries, involving relevant

intergovernmental and international organizations and forums, to investigate and make proposals for action, as appropriate, on the governance of Internet by 2005.

> World Summit on the Information Society, Geneva
> Declaration of Principles, WSIS-03/GENEVA/DOC/0004,
> 12 December 2003, 12 December 2004.

The Geneva Plan of Action, which had been negotiated in parallel with the Declaration, was more explicit on the terms of reference of the Working Group. The Plan of Action stated:

> We ask the Secretary General of the United Nations to set up a working group on Internet governance, in an open and inclusive process that ensures a mechanism for the full and active partici-pation of governments, the private sector and civil society from both developing and developed countries, involving relevant inter-governmental and international organizations and forums, to investigate and make proposals for action, as appropriate, on the governance of Internet by 2005.
>
> World Summit on the Information Society, Geneva Plan of Action,
> WSIS-03/GENEVA/DOC/0005, 12 December 2004, para. 13(b)

The Plan said that the group should develop a working definition of Internet governance, identify the public policy issues that are relevant to Internet governance, and develop a common understanding of the respective roles and responsibilities of governments, existing inter-governmental and international organizations and other forums, as well as the private sector and civil society from both developing and developed countries. The group should prepare a report on the results of this activity to be presented for consideration and appropriate action for the second phase of WSIS in Tunis in 2005.

In some respects, the agreement was revolutionary. First, the Working Group on Internet Governance, soon to be known by its acronym WGIG (pronounced Wigig), was to be a multi-stakeholder body. Second, rather than being an intergovernmental body, it was to be organized by the United Nations secretary-general, thus providing both the legitimacy of the United Nations as an organization but avoiding the legal differences in status between state and non-state actors.

The Geneva summit essentially gave two tasks to the Tunis summit, Internet governance and financing for ICTs for Development. While financing was an old issue that appeared at all development-related international meetings, Internet governance was completely new.

Civil society seemed to have been surprised by the agreement to create the WGIG. The caucus of civil society organizations presented a declaration to the summit on 8 December which, among other things, stated that WSIS should give special attention to improving the global coordination of the Internet's underlying resources. However, it opposed a purely intergovernmental model and argued that "only a truly open, multistakeholder, and flexible approach can ensure the Internet's continued growth and transition into a multilingual medium." It also called for the replacement of ICANN—without naming it—by "a global, multistakeholder entity."[15]

Preparations for WSIS II

As with most international meetings that reach an unexpected agreement, there is a period in which international organizations have to organize themselves to take up the new tasks. When the summit decision was made, no "statement of program budget implications" was made. In the United Nations, before any intergovernmental decision is made, the secretariat is supposed to indicate how much it will cost. This is to prevent decisions to accumulate that increase the amount of funds that states have to pay as part of their assessed contributions to the United Nations. If a statement of implications had been made, consensus on the text would not have been reached because the United States and probably Japan as well would have objected on the grounds of cost. However, by not making the statement, the secretary-general would have to find other sources of funding for WGIG.

ITU expert group

While WGIG was being created, very slowly, other entities began to address the issue of Internet governance. The first out of the starting blocks was the International Telecommunications Union. ITU organized an expert meeting on 26–27 February 2004. It was organized quickly in order to establish ITU's credentials in the field. It made an effort to achieve a multi-stakeholder balance.

Some 140 persons came, including governments, private sector and civil society. Included among paper presenters were many of the government officials and civil society activists who had worked on Internet governance in the WSIS process. One was Markus Kummer from the Swiss foreign ministry, who had been responsible for facilitating the agreement that led to the WGIG. Others included Wolfgang Kleinwächter, Milton Mueller, Karl Auerbach, Ayesha Hassan, Bertrand de la Chapelle, William Drake, Izumi Aizu and Bob Kahn. The keynote paper was prepared by Don MacLean and was entitled "Herding Schrödinger's Cats: Some Conceptual Tools for Thinking about Internet Governance." MacLean is a Canadian who has worked in strategic planning in the telecommunications sector. His title, as he put it, was intended to be provocative: "The expression 'herding cats' refers to a task that is very difficult, perhaps impossible, to accomplish—a good description of the challenge of coordinating the Internet-related interests and activities of governments, the private sector, civil society, and international organizations." As he explained, "Schrödinger's cat" was the subject of a famous thought experiment by an Austrian physicist which demonstrated that absurd results can follow if principles that make sense in one context are applied to very different kinds of problems. MacLean said that this was "a suitable caution for all those grappling with the complexities of Internet governance!"[16]

The result of the discussion, in the form of a chairperson's statement, was to indicate some beginnings of a consensus. One was that Internet governance could not be dealt with inside a single international organization. The other was that there were competing definitions, where some focused only on governance as technical and the other on governance as involving public policy issues. His conclusion was that a definition of Internet governance would be difficult.

The ITU event focused on what might be called the Geneva part of the UN system. Government delegates were mostly from the Permanent Missions there and most of the civil society participants were from Europe.

UN-ICT Task Force Global Forum on Internet Governance

A second event was, in some sense, a counter-conference. It was a meeting organized by the United Nations ICT Task Force. The ICT Task Force had been created as a result of the ECOSOC discussion in 2000 and, like the proposal for WGIG, was under the patronage of the UN secretary-general and therefore involved governments, the private sector and civil society. It was funded from extra-budgetary sources, raised from both governments and the private sector, and was being chaired by Jose Maria Figueres, the former president of Costa Rica. Its executive secretary was Sarbuland Khan, who also directed the Division for Economic and Social Council Support and Coordination. It was part of the UN's input into WSIS and had a terms of reference that carried it through to the Tunis summit.

The meeting, called the Global Forum on Internet Governance, was held at UN headquarters in New York from 25–26 March 2004. It drew a slightly different participant group than ITU in Geneva and clearly intended to engage the New York UN delegations and the U.S. Internet industry in the governance debate. At the same time, the main participants were familiar faces. The forum started with a briefing from Vint Cerf on the technical dimensions of the Internet (from which the graphics in Chapter 1 are taken). Don MacLean's paper on "Herding Schrödinger's Cats" was on the agenda, as was a paper by William Drake. APC's Anriette Esterhuyzen chaired one panel and Karen Banks was rapporteur on another. Reports on progress in Geneva were presented by Markus Kummer and Bertrand de la Chapelle.

The forum had a precedent-setting impact at UN headquarters in that the normal protocol of meetings was that governments sit in front, international organizations sit behind governments and non-governmental organizations and other observers sit in the back. The normal protocol also says that governments speak first, then international organizations and only when there is time, the non-state participants. The forum had free seating, no name-plates and no fixed speaking order. In some respects, it was the kind of multi-stakeholder approach that many civil society advocates had envisaged.

The forum was attended by 302 persons. About 35 percent were from governments, 14 percent from international organizations, 18 percent from the private sector, and 33 percent from civil society. The roster included most of the people who subsequently became major actors in setting up the Internet Governance Forum.

The forum reached no formal conclusions. An informal summary prepared by the ICT Task Force secretariat merely specified what was said. Several consequences ensued, however. The format of the forum worked well in the opinion of all participants, including the government representatives. To the extent that Geneva delegations are influenced by New York procedures this made subsequent innovations in Geneva easier. Second, the ICT Task Force produced a number of analytical papers in a volume edited by Don MacLean, including his "Schrödinger's Cats" piece, that was available by September 2004. Called *Internet Governance: A Grand Collaboration*, it set the tone that Internet governance was essentially a positive rather than a negative thing. The documents were made available over the Internet and a subsequent study showed that they had been extensively downloaded even among those who were not present. Subsequently, the UN-ICT Task Force sponsored the production of a series of analytical papers that sought to define the issues to be dealt with in the negotiations process.

One of these papers, "Internet Governance: The State of Play," was prepared by the Internet Governance Project, an academic consortium run out of Syracuse University.[17] It was an analysis of the extent to which issues in different regimes overlapped and existing governance arrangements might be coming into play with the Internet.

WGIG

The first PrepCom for the Tunis summit was held in Tunisia from 24–26 June 2004. This provided an incentive for the United Nations to appoint a secretariat for the WGIG. Absent any regular funding for the secretariat and for the WGIG itself, it was dependent on voluntary funding. Having invested in the Geneva summit, the government of Switzerland provided funds for the secretariat and, since he had been the lead negotiator in the process leading to the creation of WGIG, Markus Kummer was named Excecutive Coordinator of the WGIG. His office began work on 1 July 2004 and they scheduled the first consultation on the organization of WGIG in September 2004.

Nitin Desai was named by the secretary-general to chair the WGIG and it began to acquire a small staff. In fact, other than Markus Kummer, the only other staff member was Chengetai Massango, a specialist in information studies from Zambia who was completing a Ph.D. at Syracuse University. Funding primarily came from the Swiss government, but the secretariat also received funding from France, the Netherlands, Norway and Japan, as well as the Numbers Resource Organization, the Swiss Education and Research Network (SWITCH), ICANN and the Foundation for MultiMedia Communications. It could be argued, therefore, that the funding of the secretariat was also multi-stakeholder.

Because precedents were being set, the secretariat decided to move slowly to ensure that there was a consensus on the structure of the working group. A consultation was organized in Geneva from 20–21 September 2004. Attended by over 165 governmental, 52 intergovernmental organizations, 19 business and 44 NGO participants (including academics), it was organized around a series of panels that involved many of the persons who had been involved in both ICANN and WSIS. The three panels had a careful balance between government, private sector and civil society. Government representatives came from Egypt, Brazil, Tunisia, China and Japan. William Drake, Jovan Kurilja of the Diplo Foundation in Geneva, and Milton Mueller provided an academic perspective. Reflecting stakeholder views were Ayesha Hassan of the International Chamber of Commerce, Karen Banks from the Association for Progressive Communications, London, Olivier Nana Nzépa for Africa Civil Society from Cameroon, and Dr. Hans Falk Hoffmann from CERN, Geneva.

A key panel focused on the structure and composition of WGIG. There was a government representative from Brazil and from Japan. An Internet Society (ISOC) representative was the third presenter and the final one was Jeannette Hoffman, representing a formal civil society Internet governance coalition. The coalition was similar to that organized before the Geneva WSIS summit. It operated by trying to obtain a consensus of its many members. Hoffman had been (and would continue to be) an important participant in the WGIG process and beyond.

The final session of the consultation was an open debate. Following the precedent that everyone could speak, there were 21 government interventions, 9 from the private sector, 7 from international organizations and 10 from civil society. A major consideration was whether the WGIG would take a broad or a narrow view of what is covered by governance. The consensus was to take a wider view. Another issue was the size of the WGIG. There was a need to balance the need for representativeness against the practicalities of process in which when there are more parties, negotiation is longer and more complex. In the United Nations, states tend to negotiate through groups (such as the Group of 77, the European Union, and a loose group including the non-European developed countries called JUSCANZ[18]), but this would not be the case for WGIG where all of the members were formally working in their individual capacities.

At the end of the consultation, Desai concluded that[19]

> There is a general feeling that the composition of the WGIG should be balanced. Different views were held as to how this balance could be achieved and it is clear that we are looking at a balance across different dimensions. Among the considerations put forward were regional representation, stakeholders, gender, developed and developing countries, and differing schools of thought.

He went on to say that there was a widespread consensus that the process should be open, transparent and inclusive; that WGIG was expected to be different from classical expert groups; and that an innovative approach would be needed to meet expectations. With regard to the composition of the WGIG, he noted the different views, but said that there seemed to be a consensus that it should have between 30 and 40 members and that they should be working or expert level persons. He concluded that "What we are looking for is a group that is being accepted as being representative by governments and all stakeholders."

The WGIG was constructed by the secretariat using very informal means of consultation. The United Nations has become very adept at creating expert bodies that are balanced. The extent to which they succeeded in terms of the criteria set out by Desai is shown in Table 7.3. There was a good balance between stakeholder types, although the largest group consisted of governments. There was a balance between different regions, and developed and developing countries. They did not do as well on gender. As to "differing schools of thought," the mix of participants, which in the civil society component included academics as well as activists, certainly included different approaches to the issue. For example, both William Drake and Wolfgang Kleinwächter were appointed, as was Alyesha Hassan of the International Chamber of Commerce. Peng Hwa Ang, a professor from Singapore, had just completed a study entitled *Ordering Chaos: Regulating the Internet*.[20] All had been involved in WSIS from the beginning. There were participants with experience in ICANN, like Alejandro Pisanty and Avri Doria, and others who came out of the development area. A number of participants were clearly suggested by governments, although they would serve in their individual capacity. There were a number of experts who were from the United States but none from the U.S. government, which preferred to maintain its distance.

Once the WGIG was named, it began a series of meetings intended to lead it to a conclusive report. The first was held in Geneva from 23–25 November 2004. It had one day of open consultations and two days of closed meetings. A large number of governments participated, mostly through Geneva delegations, but relatively few civil society or private sector entities were represented. The first meeting decided on an outline to follow for the report and agreed on a procedure to receive input. A number

Table 7.3 Composition of the WGIG by type

Africa	7	18%
Asia and the Pacific	8	21%
Europe	12	31%
Latin America and the Caribbean	8	21%
North America	4	10%
Developed	16	41%
Developing	23	59%
Governments	17	44%
Non-governmental	11	28%
Private sector	11	28%
Female	4	10%
Male	35	90%

of the participants, especially the academics, prepared papers for the session. In that way, the WGIG was set up as a learning process. It also meant that there would be a particularly important role for the academics in the group.

The model of an open consultation followed by a closed meeting was followed for the rest of the process. Desai as chair would make summaries that were used as means to move ahead. The consultations began to be broadcast over the Internet itself, by streaming verbatim text, which made the process increasingly transparent.

The WGIG was essentially asked to answer three questions: what is Internet governance, what are the public policy issues included in Internet governance and what should be done next. It went directly to work on the first question. By the end of its second meeting, in February 2005, there were two alternative definitions, called respectively descriptive and prescriptive:[21]

First descriptive sentence: Internet governance means the collective rules, procedures, and related programs intended to shape social actors' expectations, practices, and interactions concerning Internet infrastructure and transactions and content.

Second prescriptive sentence: Internet governance should be multilateral, transparent and democratic, with the full and balanced involvement of governments, the private sector, civil society and international organizations. It should encompass both technical and public policy aspects, ensure an equitable distribution of resources, facilitate access for all, and maintain the stable and secure functioning of the Internet, taking into account multilingualism.

The descriptive definition had been proposed by Bill Drake and reflected international regime theory. The prescriptive description was drawn from the agreed text of the Geneva Plan of Action. At the same time, the initial list of public policy issues was fairly long, but these were summarized into four groups: equitable distribution of resources; access for all; stable and secure functioning of the Internet; and multilingualism and content, and other issues for consideration.[22]

The secretariat worked with the WGIG to set in motion an extensive process of public consultation. For the session from 18–20 April 2005, WGIG members prepared a series of 12 papers covering the issues in the four clusters that had been determined in February. These were intended to be factual assessments of the issues involved in each of the clusters. Written comments and proposals were solicited from interested stakeholders. Thirty-four different written comments were received, four from governments and six from international organizations. Eight contributions came from private sector organizations—including domain name registrars, the International Chamber of Commerce and trade associations representing publishers and the motion picture industry. Nine NGO submissions were received, including three from different groups within the WSIS civil society working groups, and there were seven individual contributions. There was again an open consultation where WGIG members interacted with others, and major statements were made by the government of Japan, the presidency of the European Union, the Internet Society of China and the Internet Governance Task Force of Japan.

The first stage of contributions suggested some of the difficulties that would be faced. One of these had to do with intellectual property, where the private sector representatives did not want the issue to be considered as part of Internet governance but instead remain with WIPO and the WTO, while NGOs wanted the issue included because of its connection with broader concepts of openness and access.

During its deliberations, the WGIG began to consider the follow-up to WSIS. It developed a questionnaire for interested parties in which it suggested four possible functions for the follow-up mechanisms. These included a forum function to provide a space for different stakeholders to examine aspects of Internet governance for which there was no existing institution, an oversight function—particularly for critical Internet resources, a coordination function at the managerial level, and a function mutually adjusting national and global arrangements.

WGIG members filled in the questionnaire and a summary of their replies was presented on 1 June 2005.[23] It pointed out that there was an emerging consensus on the need for a forum function but not on the type of institution to provide the forum. There was no consensus on the other functions, especially that of oversight. The questionnaire received 11 responses from others, including five from governments or groups of governments (the African group). Almost all were supportive of the forum idea, while there was no consensus on the other functions.

The process of receiving comments and consulting by Internet means continued until the final meeting of WGIG from 14–17 June 2005. As in previous meetings, an open consultation was held on 14 June, where a large number of interventions were made by key governments (Brazil, China, India, Pakistan—on behalf of the Group of 77, Nicaragua—on behalf of the Latin American and Caribbean States, Saudi Arabia, Syria), ICANN (including its CEO, Paul Twomey), the IETF, the W3C, a number of non-governmental organizations and individuals. There was a general consensus, again, about the value of a forum, but no clear consensus on how it should be organized nor on its status. Brazil, for example, would have liked to have it established through an international convention, while others wanted it less formal. Some states again wanted to create oversight over ICANN, while ICANN resisted this. There was a clear consensus that a forum should be multi-stakeholder in composition.

The WGIG then went into a two-day retreat. As part of its operating mode, it used what is called the Chatham House Rule, drawn from the practice of the Royal Institute of International Affairs whose head-quarters is Chatham House in London. The purpose of the rule is to allow people to speak as individuals, and to express views that may not be those of their organizations, and therefore it encourages free discussion. People usually feel more relaxed if they don't have to worry about their reputation or the implications if they are publicly quoted. The rule reads "When a meeting, or part thereof, is held under the Chatham House Rule, participants are free to use the information received, but neither the identity nor the affiliation of the speaker(s), nor that of any other participant, may be revealed."[24]

The importance of the Chatham House Rule for a multi-stakeholder group rests with the fact that government representatives, particularly, could participate actively and could, if necessary, accept agreements that would be difficult in a public event. The same is true of most informal negotiations in the United Nations, but these do not involve non-state participants.

Nitin Desai described the process in a remarkable book on WGIG prepared by its members:[25]

> Well before the group met in Chateau de Bossey in June 2005, it had developed a camaraderie and team spirit. People knew one another and what they could expect in an argument. There was a real sense of ownership, and a commitment to get an agreed report despite the differences that remained. The atmosphere in the Chateau helped in promoting a certain *bonhomie*. The group members, thrown together not just for the meetings but also for all meals and convivial evenings in the fine garden, became friends who had differences on substantive matters but who were prepared to find a way through out of a sense of responsibility and friend-ship. The discussions at the Chateau were intense and tempers occasionally frayed. My job as the chair was to keep the process moving, cajole people toward compromise, lighten the mood when the going got rough, and once in a while simulate anger! But the

Group members rose to the task and practically everyone pitched in contributing some text to the final product.

The resulting report reflected a consensus that was largely consistent with what had been evolving in the consultation process. There was agreement on the definition of Internet governance noted in Chapter 1. There was agreement on a list of public policy issues that was inclusive. In terms of institutional arrangements, however, there was less agreement. The forum idea was endorsed, based on the open consultation process experience of the WGIG, supported by a very lightweight structure and guided by a multi-stakeholder coordinating process, to be defined. It should avoid duplication with existing institutions and make use of research and work carried out by others.[26]

With regard to the oversight function, where the target was obviously ICANN, there was no consensus and WGIG produced four alternatives, ranging from an intergovernmental institution—favored by governments like Brazil, to nothing—favored by ICANN. The WGIG did agree, as principles, that any organizational form for the governance function/oversight function should adhere to the principles that no single government should have a pre-eminent role in relation to international Internet governance; and that it should be multilateral, transparent and democratic, with the full involvement of governments, the private sector, civil society and international organizations, participating according to their roles. The last two notions were drawn from the WSIS Declaration of Principles and were therefore "agreed text," but the first one, in effect rejecting U.S. hegemony in the management of core resources, was new.

Final PrepComs

The three PrepComs, as well as the WGIG consultations, had been well attended. As Figure 7.1 shows, there was a growth in attendance over the period, both of governments and, especially, of civil society entities. By the final preparatory committee meeting, the largest group present was from civil society.

The WGIG report became the basis of the final negotiations for the Tunis summit. A large number of governments, private sector entities and non-governmental organizations commented on the report. The major issues were the oversight mechanisms and the forum structure. The secretariat prepared a section-by-section compilation of the comments.[27] The comments came from 13 governments (including a contribution from the 25 EU states plus two acceding member states, and

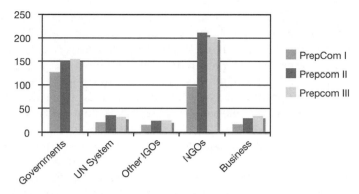

Figure 7.1 Participation by different entities in the Tunis summit Preparatory Committee meetings.

from Ghana for the Africa region), 10 business entities, 3 international organizations, 16 civil society and non-governmental organizations, and 8 miscellaneous contributions, including members of the WGIG.

The comments suggested considerable consensus about most of the report, including the forum idea. There was, however, still no consensus on oversight. With regard to the forum idea, there were unanswered questions regarding the authority of the forum, although it was clear that there would be a consensus that it should be open, with a small secretariat, and multi-stakeholder in composition, as the WGIG had recommended. There was less clarity about what it would do. As the comment from the Internet Governance Project (based at Syracuse University) put it:

> The consensus notion of a multi-stakeholder forum suggests that further discussion, debate and negotiation should take place. This can build on the growing body of analysis that informed the WGIG work, but clearly must be given a greater sense of direction. The forum, therefore, has to be seen as a preparatory element for something else.

The "something else" was left to the forum itself to define, as will be seen in Chapter 8.

The United States, which had kept some distance from the WGIG, continued to protect the ICANN model and resist intergovernmental oversight of the critical Internet resources.

The Preparatory Committee that met from 19–30 September 2005 in Geneva was not able to resolve the governance issues and as a result the Preparatory Committee had to resume its meeting in Tunis from 13–15 November 2005, just before the start of the summit itself. At the end of the September session, the chair of the subcommittee concerned with the governance text prepared a "chairman's food for thought paper" to try to work around the conflicts. At this point in any negotiation the main parties are governments rather than non-state actors, although at the end of the September session a number of non-state actors provided proposals. The chair's proposals included the idea of "an Inter-Governmental Council for global public policy and oversight of Internet governance." The suggested council, if it were established, "should be based on the principles of transparency and democracy with the involvement, in an advisory capacity, of the private sector, civil society and the relevant inter-governmental and international organisations."[28] This idea had little chance of success because the private sector and civil society would have difficulties accepting only an advisory role and many governments would have difficulty with the advisory role, period. The paper also proposed, for the first time, that the secretary-general be requested to "examine the establishment of a new space for policy dialogue—Internet Governance Forum (IGF)—initially for a period of five years."

The idea of an Inter-Governmental Council died almost instantly given the opposition of the United States. As part of a compromise, the idea of the Internet Governance Forum (IGF) grew and became more specific. The final text formally requested the secretary-general to convene the IGF in 2006 and set out some specific tasks and constraints.

The agreed text of the Tunis Agenda for the Information Society mandated the Forum to:[29]

(a) Discuss public policy issues related to key elements of Internet governance in order to foster the sustainability, robustness, security, stability, and development of the Internet;

(b) Facilitate discourse between bodies dealing with different cross-cutting international public policies regarding the Internet and discuss issues that do not fall within the scope of any existing body;

(c) Interface with appropriate intergovernmental organizations and other institutions on matters under their purview;

(d) Facilitate the exchange of information and best practices, and in this regard make full use of the expertise of the academic, scientific, and technical communities;

(e) Advise all stakeholders in proposing ways and means to accelerate the availability and affordability of the Internet in the developing world;

(f) Strengthen and enhance the engagement of stakeholders in existing and/or future Internet governance mechanisms, particularly those from developing countries;

(g) Identify emerging issues, bring them to the attention of the relevant bodies and the general public, and, where appropriate, make recommendations;

(h) Contribute to capacity building for Internet governance in developing countries, drawing fully on local sources of knowledge and expertise;

(i) Promote and assess, on an ongoing basis, the embodiment of WSIS principles in Internet governance processes;

(j) Discuss, inter alia, issues relating to critical Internet resources;

(k) Help to find solutions to the issues arising from the use and misuse of the Internet, of particular concern to everyday users;

(l) Publish its proceedings.

It went on to specify that the Internet Governance Forum, "in its working and function, will be multilateral, multi-stakeholder, democratic and transparent." The proposed IGF could follow the model of the WGIG and build on existing structure, have a lightweight and decentralized structure, and meet periodically.

The agreement was to have the IGF meet for five years and then review it. The method of setting up the forum was left to the secretary-general. No statement of program budget implications was issued, again implying that financing of the forum would have to come from voluntary sources.

The net result of the Tunis summit was to provide for an innovative, if risky, effort of building a multi-stakeholder approach into public policy and governance at the international level, an experiment that could have much broader implications if successful.

8 The IGF experiment begins

The Tunis summit left much of Internet governance open for discussion. The list of problems left unresolved was fairly long. Instead, it launched an audacious experiment in multi-stakeholder governance at the international level for which there is little precedent. The Internet Governance Forum was, in many ways, a compromise between those who wanted a vigorous, authoritative and intergovernmental institution to oversee the Internet and those who wanted no oversight at all. The compromise was based on the premise that if policy questions were discussed in an open, multi-stakeholder space, they could lead to a kind of order that only a partnership between governments, the private sector and civil society could achieve. From 2006 until the end of 2007, the experiment has begun to unfold. Two forums have been held, in Athens in November 2006 and in Rio de Janeiro in 2007. They have been considered successful, but, as Jeanette Hoffman, one of those involved in advising on IGF management, put it in a private conversation, it is still fragile.

If successful, it can provide a model for similar substantive areas. If unsuccessful, it can set back the idea that governance can go beyond the nation-state. To make an appraisal, we should start by looking at the processes that have been followed in the first two years of the experiment.

Setting up the IGF

As noted, the IGF was almost the last thing agreed at Tunis. It was to be based on a model where the United Nations secretary-general acted as convener and patron. The model had been used for both the WSIS and for the Information and Communication Technology for Development Task Force. While it is not totally unprecedented in terms of the scope of its terms of reference, the IGF's approach is probably without precedent.

Having the secretary-general convene the forum is a device that allows equal status to all stakeholders, rather than establishing a hierarchy in which governments are paramount. For this to happen, governments had to accept some rather ambiguous terms of reference.

The secretariat

The Tunis agenda specified that the forum's structure should be light-weight and decentralized. Since no statement of program budget implications was given at Tunis, the assumption was that the structure would not be funded from the regular assessed budget of the organization. Instead, it would have to be funded, like the WGIG, on the basis of extra-budgetary contributions. In the end, the simplest way to do that was to convert the WGIG secretariat into the IGF secretariat with the same staff.

Markus Kummer was named executive coordinator, with Chengatai Masango as a full-time staff member on a consultant contract. The remaining staff for most of the period were interns. Nitin Desai was named chair of the forum. As a retired UN official, his cost was minimal. By United Nations standards, this was a very light secretariat.

Funds for the secretariat were provided, again, by the Swiss government, together with the governments of Norway, the Netherlands and the United Kingdom. Showing that the multi-stakeholder approach carried over to funding, resources were also received from ICANN, a number of regional and national Internet registries, Siemens, and the Verizon Foundation. The funding base, however, is not secure.

The consultations

At the Tunis summit, Greece had offered to host the first forum, so the venue was known in advance. However, there were few precedents for organizing the forum and as a first step, as had been customary, the United Nations organized a two-day consultation in February 2006 in Geneva. It was well attended, with 44 governments, mostly from Geneva missions, 10 intergovernmental organizations and 109 non-state organizations. The non-state participants were divided between private sector entities including the International Chamber of Commerce, Cisco Systems, ICANN, and domain name registries. They included NGOs like the Association for Progressive Communications, and the Conference of NGOs (CONGO). There were representatives of technical bodies like the Internet Society and the W3C Consortium, and there were academics like the Syracuse University based Internet

Governance Project and Wolfgang Kleinwächter of the University of Aarhus. Several of the participants had been members of the WGIG, while others had been active in the WSIS process generally.

The discussions focused on three basic questions: what issues would be discussed at Athens, how would they be discussed and who would decide this. The matter of issues revolved around whether all issues raised in the WGIG report could be considered by the forum, or whether there were going to be limitations. One element in the discussions was whether issues that presumably were dealt with in existing institutions, like intellectual property (by WIPO and WTO) should be taken up. Another was whether management of the root servers was an issue to be discussed.

Since there was no real precedent for the forum, the issue of how to discuss issues was a matter of some concern. The standard UN method would be to have all substantive discussions in plenary meetings with interpretation into all of the official languages. At UN conferences, the possibility existed for outside events that could take up other issues. In fact, at many UN conferences the outside events were predictors of the issues that might be taken up at conference follow-ups. The problem for the forum was that plenaries are costly, because of the need for interpretation and, based on sequences of speakers, can be deadly boring. In some bodies, panel discussions had been added to try to relieve the deadliness of the proceedings. Most of the speakers pushed for an open approach to structuring the forum, not excluding any issues. Some governments were keen to keep a plenary discussion.

Finally, on the decision-making, some governments pushed for a group that would make procedural decisions. Their model was the traditional bureau structure, where government representatives, regionally balanced, would agree on matters. At WSIS there had been three bureaus, one for governments, another for the private sector, and a third for non-governmental organizations. In practice the government bureau dominated and the other groups did not like the bureau idea. The notion that the management group could be constructed like the WGIG, which had demonstrably worked well, had considerable support.

At the end of the session, in what was to become a common practice, Nitin Desai, as chair, sought to pluck consensus from the air. Having been the secretary-general's representative at a large number of international conferences, Desai was remarkably good at sensing the kind of language that all participants would accept. Included in this was insisting that the summary did not represent an agreement, but rather ideas that had found some favor if one looked at the discussions. This process was helped by the fact that, in order to make the proceedings available over the Internet in real time, the entire discussions, as had been done for WGIG, were transcribed. The transcriptions have been maintained on the IGF web site.

On the issues to discuss, Desai concluded that they would be constrained by the number of days and available facilities in Athens and three themes would probably be all that would fit.[1]

In terms of how the forum would be organized, he again used an argument based on time and space. He suggested a plenary space "which would allow the entire—all of the people attending, or a substantial portion of those attending, to participate in this—the major thematic discussions over these days." In addition, he proposed "space for smaller meetings, panel discussions, roundtables, working groups." These would be linked to the themes but would be organized by different constituencies. Finally, he proposed a "learning space" where presentations could be made of best practices and innovations.

He did not sense a consensus about how to construct what he called the "management group," although he said that it was clear that it should be multi-stakeholder. With that in mind he left the matter open.

At the end of the session, the Brazilian delegate took the floor and offered to hold the 2007 session of the forum in Brazil. After the consultations, the secretariat prepared a paper summarizing the themes that had been suggested. The secretariat's role in these kinds of negotiations is to structure proposals received in such a way that they can be agreed, without at the same time implying that it endorses them. The list of issues was fairly long and far-ranging and included spam, multilingualism, cybercrime, cybersecurity, privacy and data protection, freedom of expression and human rights, international connection costs, finance and e-commerce. In short most of the issues that were still contentious.[2] The issues not included were also interesting: critical Internet resources and intellectual property.

Although at the end of the session Desai had indicated that a new consultation would not be possible, in fact the secretariat organized another one in May 2006. Following the practice of the WGIG, the consultation was organized just before a meeting of what was called the Multistakeholder Advisory Group, the management group that Desai had mentioned in February. Based on further consultations, with governments and the various caucuses, the secretariat had proposed— and the secretary-general's office had confirmed—a list of names.

The May consultation continued the discussion of issues. Brazil, for example, reiterated the need to discuss critical Internet resources. The need for multi-stakeholder approaches was emphasized. The Indian delegate announced his country's offer to host the 2008 forum in Delhi.

The MAG

The 47-member Multistakeholder Advisory Group (MAG) became the management group that Desai had mentioned in February. It was truly multi-stakeholder in composition. Table 8.1 shows the distribution of the 46 members (Desai, as chair, was the 47th member). Almost half of the members were from governments. A third of the members were from the private sector. NGOs and members of the technical constituencies (ISOC, IETF, and W3C) made up a quarter. About two-fifths of the members were from Western Europe, North America, and Australia and New Zealand (the Western European and Other group). If the members from Eastern Europe are added, exactly half of the members were from developed countries.

The members included familiar names like Ayesha Hassan of the International Chamber of Commerce, Adam Peake, Jeanette Hoffman, and Robin Gross from the civil society caucus. Thirteen percent of the members (six) had been on the ICANN staff or board. Only 13 percent were women, none of these from the government members.

The MAG met twice before Athens in 2006. The first time, in May, it agreed on the broad structure of the agenda, and in a second meeting, in September, it agreed on the panelists and the specific working groups. The structure of the Athens meeting, which carried over to the Rio meeting, was fairly nuanced.

There would be plenary discussions of broad issue clusters. These were defined as openness, security, diversity and access. They were considered to be cross-cutting. In addition, there would be workshops organized by different groups that would focus on specific issues. There would be no

Table 8.1 Composition of the Multistakeholder Advisory Group (MAG) by constituency and region, May 2006

Constituency/region	Africa	Asia and the Pacific	Eastern Europe	Latin America and the Caribbean	Western Europe and other	Grand total	N
Government	38%	50%	100%	60%	28%	46%	21
Non-governmental organizations	25%	20%	0%	0%	17%	15%	7
Private sector	25%	30%	0%	20%	44%	30%	14
Technical	13%	0%	0%	20%	11%	9%	4
Grand total	17%	22%	11%	11%	39%	100%	46
N	8	10	5	5	18	46	

formal outcome of the forum, although a summary of the discussions would be prepared by the secretariat. Space would be provided for the workshop organizers to report to the plenary. As one outcome, the MAG decided that a concept of "dynamic coalitions" could emerge, defined as a group of institutions or people who agree to pursue an initiative started at the inaugural IGF meeting. Workshop organizers were encouraged to have multi-stakeholder panels, to provide for diversity.

IGF I: Athens 2006

For anyone used to United Nations conferences, the IGF in Athens was unusual from the beginning. The government of Greece took full responsibility for organizing it, including most of the costs. Rather than place it at a usual conference center, the IGF took place at a hotel in the southern part of Athens. The forum developed in ballrooms and conference rooms. Because it was a UN conference, UN security was in charge. But there were no halls with government nameplates and participants from different groups mingled.

More than 1,200 persons were registered for the forum, including 90 government delegations. The official breakdown in participants by constituency is shown in Figure 8.1, where the breadth of participation is evident. In terms of geographical distribution, over half of the participants were from Europe, but two-fifths of these were from Greece, which usually happens since it is easier for residents of the host country to attend a conference, especially one that has open admission. A third

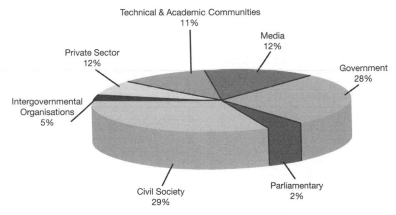

Figure 8.1 IGF Athens meeting participation by stakeholder group.
Source: www.intergovforum.org/Athens_stats_stakeholder.php

of the participants were from developing regions and 12 percent from North America.

The forum's basic structure is shown in Table 8.2. The forum was organized around plenary sessions and workshops. There were plenary sessions on security, openness, diversity and access, as well as an introductory session called "setting the scene" and two concluding sessions, one called "the way forward" and another called "emerging issues." The plenary sessions had a common, and somewhat unusual, format. For each session there was a panel of up to 10 experts, drawn from all of the stakeholder groups. Rather than the usual format at the UN of having each panelist make a presentation, the sessions were moderated by media professionals who used the format of a television program in which the moderator tries to maintain a flow of discussion by calling on different panelists, allowing them to cross-comment, and inviting the audience to join in the debate.

The first session, called "Setting the Scene," illustrates the process. The panelists, from all stakeholder groups and most regions, included representatives from civil society (like Karen Banks from the Association for Progressive Communications), from eight governments (including the United States, France and China), and from the private sector (including Paul Twomey from ICANN). The panel was moderated by Ken Cukier, a reporter for the *Economist* who had specialized in the Internet while a fellow at Harvard University's Berkman Center. Subsequent panels had a similar pattern of participants and were moderated by professionals from the BBC, the Japan Broadcasting Corporation and France 24.

The panels were all webcast and there were real-time transcripts of all of the sessions. In practice, the discussions were lively and well attended. In the plenary session on openness, panelists from Cisco Systems and Google were questioned from the floor about whether their corporate

Table 8.2 Structure of the Athens Forum, 2006

October 30	October 31	November 1	November 2
Opening ceremony	Openness session	Summing up	Summing up
Setting the scene	Security session	Diversity session	The way forward
			...
		Access session	Emerging issues session
			Closing ceremony

policies were helping China suppress content. Other discussants raised the issues of attempts to censor YouTube and MySpace.

Much of the work of the forum took place in the 36 working groups that were organized by different stakeholders. They covered a variety of themes. In practice, any stakeholder that wanted to organize a working group was allowed to do so, after having been vetted for legitimacy. Built into the process was the possibility of reporting back to the plenary, which many of the workshops did. An example is the report by Jeanette Hoffman of the Internet Governance Project on a workshop on content filtering and freedom of expression that concluded "that the universal declaration of human rights still provides the best framework possible to both enable and protect freedom of speech on the Internet, not least because it is very clear and specific about acceptable restrictions on freedom of speech." She noted that the workshop had not been able to conclude whether self-regulation by industry was sufficient or whether government action was required.[3]

One of the expected outcomes of the forum was the formation of "dynamic coalitions," groups of stakeholders that would work on specific issues identified in the Athens forum that could be carried forward to subsequent forums. A number emerged, including dynamic coalitions on privacy, an Internet Bill of Rights and gender. One had to do with a framework convention, and this is an example of how the process is working.

One problem with Internet governance as a concept, as has been noted throughout this study, is that there is no natural institutional home for all of the issues that are involved. Moreover, the process of agreeing on institutional arrangements was assumed from the beginning to be long and complex. Given that in most international agreements, the most complex negotiations have to do with institutional nuts and bolts rather than broader issues of principles and norms, I had suggested in 1998 that consideration be given to elaborating a framework convention similar to that which had started the global process of dealing with climate change.[4] After the Internet governance issue had emerged again after the Geneva phase of WSIS, I had written another article arguing for a Framework Convention on Internet Governance, that was distributed by the Internet Governance Project and had been widely read.[5]

A group of stakeholders organized a workshop at the forum under the title "Exploring a Framework Convention on the Internet." The sponsors were mostly NGOs from developing countries and included IT for Change, Bangalore; Hivos, Netherlands; Panos Institute, West Africa—CIPACO Project; Third World Institute (ITeM), Uruguay; and the Foundation for Media Alternatives, Philippines. The panel had government, private sector, NGO and academic members and included Parminder Jeet Singh (IT for Change); John Mathiason (Internet Governance Project, Syracuse University); William Drake (Graduate Institute of International Studies in Geneva); Pankaj Agrawala (Joint Secretary, Ministry of IT, India); Erick Iriarte Ahon (Alfa-Redi); and Bertrand de la Chappelle (the French government's Special Envoy for the Information Society).

The panelists did not reach a consensus on the idea. Some favored a convention, while others, especially William Drake, argued that "that a Convention is only suitable for inter-governmental arrangements and that as internet governance was committed to a multi-stakeholder process we will need to think beyond the existing international law instruments." He suggested that it was futile to think in terms of a single body of general principles that could respond to the hetero-geneous and distributed character of the Internet and expressed a concern that such a statement of general principles could freeze the technological development of the Internet, and further Internet law and policy may end up not being responsive to the local contexts and concerns which drive its adoption and acceptability.[6] This was an argument often advanced by civil society activists against any regulation of the Internet.

With the lack of agreement on the panel about a convention, a con-sensus was reached to create a dynamic coalition. This was reported to the plenary in the session on "The Way Forward" and announced, as did other dynamic coalitions, that they would work on their issues before the Rio forum.

At the end of the forum, there were two sessions intended to provide a form of closure. The first was "The Way Forward" that was intended to summarize what had been discussed and guide the next forum. Much of this was devoted to a summary presented by Markus Kummer on behalf of the secretariat, based on the reports of the working groups as well as notes taken during the plenary sessions. The report did not draw conclusions as such, was intended more as a record, and was published on the Internet Governance Forum web site, where most of the IGF material was posted.[7]

The consensus of the speakers in the final sessions was that the forum had been successful in the sense that there was open discussion and exchange of views across stakeholder lines. Summarizing this at the closing session, Nitin Desai stated:

> And the message that we are sending out is that this—the one thing this agora [the Greek forum for public discussion] wants is

an Internet for all, the poor, the disabled, women, people in remote areas, people who do not use English as a language, people who are not familiar with the Latin script, and that if the Internet is to realize its full potential, it must be an Internet which truly is accessible, usable, and safe for all. This, I think, is the basic message that we have got from this forum.

Prior to the forum, Egypt had offered to host the 2009 forum and at the closing session, both Lithuania and Azerbaijan offered to host the 2010 session (which would belong, according to UN geographical rotation, to the Eastern European group).

On to Rio

While there was a certain amount of euphoria about the results of the Athens Forum, there were concerns that this was merely a reflection of the newness and innovation of the forum function. It was not certain that there were clear directions about where the forum was going. The Internet Governance Project, for example, issued another of its concept papers arguing that a results-based management approach should be applied to planning successive forums so that there was a clear view about what the forum should accomplish. The IGP paper suggested that by 2010 there should be some clear results in that the discussions should narrow the issues to those that would require action by states and/or other stakeholders in the appropriate formal decision-making forums, that the interrelationships among different Internet governance issues would have been explored along with new issues connected with the old ones that might emerge because of technological changes.[8]

The IGF secretariat issued a call for comments and suggestions from anyone who would be interested in taking stock of the Athens forum. With different analyses having been made of the Athens forum, the IGF secretariat convened a stock-taking session in Geneva on 13 February 2007. In advance, it prepared a paper synthesizing the comments received. Most of the comments dealt with details of organization. The stocktaking was preceded by a closed meeting of the Multistakeholder Advisory Group (MAG) and was well attended, although it was heavily composed of Europe-based organizations. The main concerns expressed were the composition of the MAG (by governments who still wanted a formal bureau structure), the need for some outcome document of each forum, as well as a sense of direction and the need to use the Internet itself to reach out to more stakeholders. Nitin Desai summarized the discussions, but the implication was that little would change for the Rio forum.

Critical Internet resources

The IGF secretariat took advantage of a series of meetings concerning WSIS follow-up in Geneva in May 2007 to organize another consultation in advance of Rio. The one-day meeting had one major highlight. The issue of critical Internet resources, revolving around ICANN, had been the genesis of the Internet governance debate in the first place. At the May consultations, led by the Latin America and Caribbean Group of States (GRULAC) at the UN but supported by civil society representatives and other governments, especially from developing countries, the great preponderance of comments called for including critical Internet resources as one of the main themes. The process by which this took place illustrates how the Internet governance approach works.

The subject had not been included in the list of those proposed by the MAG, in part because the ICANN-related members had been reluctant to accept it. The original proposal had been to have the same four themes as at Athens: Openness, Access, Diversity, and Security. There had also been a concern, expressed in February, that development aspects of Internet governance had been slighted in the forum.

Addressing this, the delegate from El Salvador speaking on behalf of GRULAC built the case for dealing with critical Internet resources around their link with the other themes, starting with the matter of capacity development in developing countries, a subject that was completely non-controversial:[9]

> With regard to contributing to capacity building for Internet governance in developing countries, taking advantage, as much as possible, of local knowledge and competencies and discussing issues relating to critical Internet resources, among other things. The forum did not touch on this issue in Athens and it is not considered in the drafts for the Rio meeting. As we said before, as far as GRULAC is concerned, topics related to critical Internet resources and the internalization of Internet governance principles are as important as access, openness, security, and diversity, and must be treated equally, although the reasons for their level of importance are different. The ideal case would be to have a fifth issue referring to Internet governance of critical resources and the attendant principles.

The GRULAC proposal was supported in statements by China, Brazil, Iran, Saudi Arabia, Chile, and the Russian Federation. It was also supported in a statement by the civil society Internet caucus, who had met beforehand to agree on a common statement, as well as by the Association for Progressive Communications and the Third World Network. Then a representative of Canada spoke in favor by suggesting that there was an emerging consensus to include the issue.

Subequently, the MAG decided to include this issue as a main theme. Thus this central issue was finally given its place in the forum.

Dynamic coalitions

The concept of dynamic coalitions that had emerged at Athens was somewhat vague. There was an implication that the coalitions would work between forums to strengthen their approaches. Some 11 dynamic coalitions had been formed dealing with spam, privacy, open standards, access and connectivity for rural and remote communities, a possible Internet Bill of Rights, linguistic diversity, general access, gender, access to knowledge, freedom of expression and, as noted earlier, a framework of principles. In the main they were organized by civil society, but in some cases governments have joined. They reflected some of the fissures in terms of issues in that dealing with spam would have implications for privacy and freedom of expression. Most were relatively passive during the transition to Rio, but at least one undertook a significant activity. This was the Dynamic Coalition on the Internet Bill of Rights.

The coalition defined itself in these terms: "the effort aims at understanding how traditional human rights can be adapted and expanded in the new online environment, and how they could be formalized in one or more documents that could act as a reference and be adopted as a code of conduct on an opt-in basis."[10] Its original members were a mixture of governments and civil society organizations including the Ministry of Culture of Brazil, the Ministry of Reform and Innovation in the Public Administration of Italy, the Centre for Technology and Society of the Getulio Vargas Foundation School of Law in Brazil, IP Justice, the Internet Society of Italy, the Free Software Foundation of Europe, the Committee for a Democratic United Nations, the Institute of International Law of the University of Graz in Austria, and the Net Dialogue Project of Harvard and Stanford Universities in the United States.

As part of the preparations for Rio, the government of Italy organized a "Dialogue Forum on Internet Rights—Italy 2007" that brought together NGOs, academics and some governments to discuss the extent to which such a bill of rights might be formed. The report of the dialogue concluded that "The issue of a better recognition and enforcement over the Internet of human rights, both existing and innovative, should be recognized as a founding and cross-cutting theme for the IGF, becoming one of its main themes for the future." It suggested the establishment of a process and framework to address this issue as an objective of the initial IGF five-year term.[11]

In addition to dynamic coalitions, other usual participants also ran their own meetings that were at least in part preparatory to Rio. For example, the Syracuse University School of Information Studies, the George Mason University Law School's Critical Infrastructure Protection Program, and the Swiss Federal Institute of Technology at Lausanne jointly organized a symposium on "Internet Governance and Security: Exploring Global and National Solutions," in Washington, D.C., in May 2007 that focused on the tensions and complementarities between global and national policy-making for issues related to the security and privacy of commerce and communication on the Internet.

A number of academics prepared papers that could help shape the Rio discussions. Milton Mueller, for example, issued an IGP paper entitled "Net Neutrality as Global Principle for Internet Governance" in early November 2007.[12] A group of academics interested in Internet governance had organized themselves at Athens as the Global Internet Governance Academic Network (GIGANET) and planned to hold another session at Rio at which research papers would be presented by scholars and discussed.

All of these events moved toward Rio. The MAG had one additional consultation, in early September 2007, to finalize the program for the forum. In addition to confirming the main themes, a "reporting back" segment was added to allow workshops to report in plenary. Session times were shortened to allow more meetings. The Brazilian hosts, having seen the space problems in Athens, made more provision for meeting rooms which allowed for more working groups. The forum was also extended to four days, and many organizations, including GIGANET, decided to meet the day before the forum formally opened.

IGF II: Rio

The 2007 Internet Governance Forum took place in Rio de Janeiro, Brazil, from 12–15 November 2007. It was a day longer than the Athens forum and was held at the Windsor Barra Hotel in the Barra district. The structure of the forum is shown in Table 8.3. The hotel had ample provision for working groups, as well as for the plenary. Of

Table 8.3 Structure of the Rio de Janeiro Forum, 2007

November 12	November 13	November 14	November 15
Opening ceremony	Reporting back session	Reporting back session	Reporting back session
Opening session	Access session	Openness session	Taking stock and the way forward
Critical Internet resources session	Afternoon reporting back session	Security session	Emerging issues
	Diversity session		Closing ceremony

the 84 events outside the plenary, there were 36 workshops, 23 best practices forums, 11 dynamic coalitions meetings, 8 open forums, and 6 events covering others issues. Of these, 11 were devoted to the issue of openness and freedom of expression, 12 on development and capacity-building, 9 on access, 10 on critical Internet resources, 6 on diversity, 17 on other issues, and 19 were devoted to the issue of security. Of the security sessions, nine spotlighted the issue of the protection of children and of child pornography on the Internet. The open forums focused on specific institutions including ICANN, ITU, UNESCO, the Internet Society and the Council of Europe. The Internet Society brought members from at least seven of its national societies.

When the meeting opened, about 1,700 participants were registered, some 500 more than at Athens. These included delegations from 90 countries. From the private sector there were participants from Alcatel-Lucent, Cisco Systems, France Telecom, Google, IBM, Intel, Microsoft, Nokia Siemens, Sun Microsystems, Verizon, and Yahoo. The International Chamber of Commerce delegation had nine members, ICANN's delegation included 19 people, and the Internet Society had 19 participants, including 10 from the Internet Society of China. The Association for Progressive Communications had a delegation of 14. Academics were well represented, including 52 faculty from different universities including Syracuse University, the Geneva Graduate Institute for International Studies, the University of Singapore, Aarhus University, Oxford University, Harvard University, the American University of Cairo and the Federal University of Santa Maria in Brazil, among others.

As in Athens, the main showcase was the plenary sessions that were translated into all official UN languages (as well as Portuguese) and were both webcast and provided with real-time transcription. In addition to the plenary sessions on openness, security, diversity and access, there was a session on critical Internet resources, and the two wrap-up sessions. The Rio program was also different from the structure in Athens in that a more concerted effort was made to allow workshops to report on their results. The purpose of doing so was to ensure that the main results were recorded as part of the official proceedings.

The opening session was designed to emphasize the multi-stakeholder nature of the forum. The speakers included the Brazilian minister of science and technology, the director-general of the ITU, the president of the Association for Progressive Communication (on behalf of civil society), the secretary-general of the International Chamber of Commerce, the president of the Internet Society, the minister of science and technology and higher education of Portugal (where Portugal had the revolving presidency of the European Union), the CEO of ICANN, the chairman of Fujitsu (the electronics corporation who was also chair of a trade association called the Global Information Infrastructure Commission), the minister of communications of South Africa, the executive secretary of the African Academy of Languages, the under secretary of communication of Italy, the vice minister for policy coordination of Japan's Ministry of Communications, the IETF liaison to the ICANN board, the deputy secretary-general of the Council of Europe, a Member of the European Parliament, the permanent secretary of the Department of Information Technology of India, and Brazil's minister of culture. The speakers were from all five major stakeholder groups (government, international organizations, civil society, the private sector and the technical community). This balance was maintained through all of the proceedings.

The first substantive session was on critical Internet resources, what has always been the heart of the matter of Internet governance. It had been avoided in the Tunis summit outcome documents and in Athens, but finally was taken up. The panel to discuss it reflected the different points of view and was chaired by Plínio de Aguiar, former president of the Brazilian federal communications regulatory agency and a board member of the Internet Steering Committee of Brazil. The moderator was Ulysse Gosset, host of the French television program *Talk de Paris*. The panel included Vint Cerf, one of the fathers of the Internet who was now a senior executive at Google and the outgoing chair of the ICANN Board; Lesley Cowley, chief executive of Nominet, the not-for-profit domain name registry for the U.K.; Alain Aina, founder and member of the African network operation group from Togo who was also a member of the ICANN security and stability committee; Milton Mueller of Syracuse University's Internet Governance Project,

Carlos Afonso, planning director of the Information Network for the Third Sector and a board member of the Internet Steering Committee for Brazil; and Raul Echeberria from Uruguay, CEO of the Latin American and Caribbean Internet Addresses Registry. Most of the panelists were old-timers who had been concerned with ICANN, either as board members or as critics. Other than the chair, no one from government was on the panel.

The panel covered many of the issues surrounding ICANN, including the usual differing perspectives on whether it should have an intergovernmental home. Its defenders argued that it was itself a multistakeholder approach and did not need to be improved, while others argued that there needed to be some form of international oversight. In the discussion, a number of relatively new issues emerged. One had to do with convergence and new regulatory structures in the context of technological change. A questioner from the audience, noting that networks are inevitably converging, asked whether there should also be institutional convergence as well.[13] Milton Mueller provided an answer that had some support from other panelists. He noted that convergence within industries does not mean different industries coming together in the same place, but rather that the Internet was taking over everything:

> So, to draw out the parallel, I would suggest that rather than seeing the ITU converge on ICANN and converge on OECD and all of the other institutions that are currently trying to in some way affect Internet governance, what you would more likely see are the growth and spread of the authority and significance of the organic Internet institutions.

He noted that ICANN's budget had grown to $50 million and that in 1998 when ICANN was created, he had predicted that within 10 years it would be the same size as the ITU. The regional Internet registries were extremely well endowed institutions, and growing stronger. He pointed out that they have a new ethic of multi-stakeholderism which was very important. Rather than convergence of the old institutions, he suggested "perhaps a more Darwinian process in which the old institutions die and the new ones grow."

Vint Cerf picked up on the point and added that when a medium moves from the traditional television world of broadcast or cable or even satellite into the Internet environment, it may not be the same kind of television that it was thought of before or that people use the medium differently. He said,

There are different opportunities for sustaining that medium, for supporting its costs, and the like. And so the regulatory oversight and structure for businesses that operate that medium in the Internet world may be quite different from the ones that may have been appropriate in other delivery mechanisms. So I think that, in my view, anyway, convergence does not necessarily endow any of the previous regulatory structures with any primacy, and, in fact, we may see completely different kinds of media arising out of this convergence with Internet delivery mechanisms. So I think, like Milton suggests, there may be a Darwinian imperative here that you either adapt to this new environment or you die.

A second point was initially posed by Plinío de Aguiar in his opening statement. It had to do with the migration of the Internet from the original protocol, IPv4, to the next one, IPv6. He said:

As regards the logic infrastructure, we have the implementation of domain names that are internationalized and the adoption of criteria for the allocation and reallocation of IP addresses and the migration of IPv4 to IPv6. All of them have a great impact on the drafting of digital inclusion public policies and the Internet in the developing world.

Commenting on this, Vint Cerf pointed out that IPv6, which was necessary because the address space in IPv4 was running out, was not backward-compatible with the previous version, meaning that a network running IPv6 could not communicate with one running on IPv4. This would have long-term implications for the extension of the Internet to developing countries, where the greatest growth is taking place.

A third issue had to do with the growth of new applications that were using the Internet, such as streaming video, that required more bandwidth. This had implications for access as well as for freedom of expression and diversity.

Finally, the issue of how governments would provide oversight focused on the Government Advisory Committee of ICANN. While ICANN representatives suggested that this was a solution to the problem of providing government input, others questioned whether governments could or should function in an advisory capacity. Milton Mueller put it most bluntly: "GAC is the wrong model. Governments should be outside ICANN, acting on an integrated basis as a check or balance." He later clarified that by bringing governments into ICANN as a so-called advisory body, you don't solve or erase the geopolitical conflicts that can prevent governments from acting on a global basis. ... What you're doing by bringing them into GAC is just reproducing all the geopolitical conflicts that already exist. And the point is, ICANN was created as a global governance agency to transcend those jurisdictional and sovereignty problems.

The chairman's summary, prepared by the secretariat, which became one of the main outcome documents of the forum, reflected these discussions. The summary concluded that there was a general recognition of the value of discussing issues such as critical Internet resources in the IGF environment. There was also recognition of the importance of building human capacity as a critical resource. Cooperation had been increasing on the issue and the spread of the multi-stakeholder methodology had proven that this was an important approach for resolving critical Internet issues.[14]

The discussion in the four other plenary sessions was rich, but seemed to cover much of the same ground as before. The reporting-back sessions provided an opportunity for specific groups, including dynamic coalitions, to reflect their concerns.

As had been done at Athens, the final substantive session dealt with emerging issues. The presentation was moderated by a BBC journalist, Nik Gowing, who was the main presenter in that network's interview program, *HARDtalk*. The discussion was free flowing, and by UN standards, very blunt. Vint Cerf, for example, referred to another panelist's presentation as "crap."[15] The discussion began to highlight issues that derived from conflicts between different aspects that had been discussed in the forum. For example, the issue of access, which everyone agreed was important, was constrained by the problems in critical Internet resources related to IPv6. The security issue of preventing misuse of Internet identities through eliminating anonymity conflicted with the value of privacy, which depended to some degree on anonymity, and with the need to protect political dissidents trying to express opinions that might conflict with governments.

Other than the official chairman's statement prepared by the IGF secretariat, there was no formal outcome document. Whether to have a formal outcome document, and what form it might take, was a matter of discussion but not resolution. Desai, in his closing-session summary, made a point about the process:[16]

One message that I do get from all of this is that in some ways, our first phase of the IGF was focused on making people a little more comfortable with each other. And that, I think, we are succeeding. And partly the reason we are succeeding is there is a certain adjustment of cultures which has taken place. Governments have been a little more willing to accept methods of discussion which are not quite what they are used to in diplomatic processes. I believe NGOs have also learned the habits of tact, if I may say that. So they realize that this is a different type of forum. And so has industry and the Internet community and the very fact that they welcome the types of debates and discussions we have had, even though often these debates have been critical of their activities, shows that we are developing a style of conversation which does lead to what I would describe as a dialogue of good faith, where people listen to each other and don't just talk at each other.

Desai expressed the hope that the dialogue could be maintained, while noting that the forum was primarily made up of people from the supply side of the Internet. He suggested increased involvement of users of the Internet, but concluded that there was evidence that the process was working.

Subsequent commentaries echoed this positive response, although with some concern. Jeanette Hoffman, an Internet Governance Project partner who was also on the MAG, noted that the process was sound, but extremely fragile because of its innovation.[17]

IGF III–V and beyond

The next stop, IGF III will be in Hyderabad and the preparations have already begun. There was the usual stocktaking event in February 2008, the MAG will have to be renewed, possibly with changes in the membership, and the IFG secretariat will report to the UN Commission on Science and Technology for Development, which has been given responsibility for monitoring the implementation of the WSIS agreements.

The prospective Hyderabad venue for the forum may be smaller than that of Rio, necessitating some changes in the structure of IGF III. Technological and political events, such as the United States presidential elections in 2008, may change the parameters of issues. However, it can be assumed that a core of the networks that have been involved with the IGF will continue in place. Of the key issues of governance noted in Chapters 1 and 3, critical Internet resources was discussed at Rio and is now on the agenda. Intellectual property and content issues other than those concerned with security, besides their theoretical connection with freedom of expression, have not yet been discussed in depth.

Still, slowly but perceptibly, the IGF has begun to narrow the issues that have to be taken up in Internet governance. To the extent that, by defining a pre-consensus on principles, the forum begins to enable governments and international organizations to see both where and how they need to reach agreements to ensure order in the global commons called the Internet, the informal process will become increasingly formal.

Sometime in 2010, before IGF V, consideration will have to be given to the future of the forum and, in the meantime, scholars and practitioners both will examine the multi-stakeholder approach set in motion for Internet governance and see whether it can be applied elsewhere.

9 What does the frontier look like?

The process of determining how to govern the Internet is a new frontier for international institutions. We can already draw some lessons from it that can help define what the frontier looks like. These lessons are both about structure and process and, based on this analysis, we can see whether there are other areas in which it can be applied. These have to do with who participates, how they reach decisions and how this connects with the larger management of solutions to global problems.

In key respects the Internet Governance Forum is not like any other current international institution. It represents a new form of global organization. Although it has a connection with the United Nations, in that it is convened under the patronage of the secretary-general, it is not an intergovernmental body in the usual sense. There are other forums, like the World Economic Forum—which has been studied in a companion volume in this series[1]—that involve leaders from government, the private sector and civil society. Unlike them, however, the IGF was created by intergovernmental decision-making, as part of the negotiations at a global summit. And unlike the World Economic Forum, where the focus is on discussing a variety of issues, built around rough annual themes, the IGF has a specific goal to achieve over an extended period of time. By bringing together, under an official United Nations umbrella, the main parties to a key element in globalization, the IGF is unique.

Who the stakeholders in Internet governance are has been largely clear from the beginning and each has defined its interests over a period. In some respects, all of them are part of the same epistemic community, to use Peter Haas' terminology.[2] As his approach would suggest, the IGF is providing policy coordination in an area where technology, economics, social forces and international norms intersect. The Internet was managed from the outset by civil society, in the form of the scientists who developed the Internet Protocol and set up rules for allowing information to flow, under a very vague and not very vigilant government stewardship. The private sector recognized its potential long before governments took an interest. It was only when the process of competition itself threatened to destabilize the network—in terms of intellectual property, crime and security concerns—that governments awoke to the need for regulation. However, while approaching the issue from different perspectives and experiences, they almost all understood the underlying technology and were able to communicate with each other, even if they did not agree. This ability to understand the underlying issues is critical to reaching agreements at the international level.

Unlike other areas where civil society, the private sector and governments interact, and where one or another stakeholder tries to achieve primacy, the IGF started with an early recognition that Internet governance, because of its borderless nature and the fact that the governance issues centered on conflicts of different international regimes, was everyone's concern but within no single actor's power. Thus, a multi-stakeholder approach has had to evolve. It is true that governments have tried to exercise their rights to regulate, by trying to maintain traditional intergovernmental structures that are based on the sovereign equality of states. The private sector has tended to take a negative view, opposing any possible regulation. Various civil society groups have had, as is always the case, different perspectives. However, these different perspectives have not stopped agreement.

A main factor in this has been the nature of agreements at the international level. In a world where formally decision-makers at the international level are sovereign states, the only way agreements can be reached is by consensus. Consensus is achieved in stages. There has to be agreement on what the facts are, and the contours of the problem to be addressed. In regime theory this is called agreement on principles. Then, there has to be agreement on the general obligations of states and other stakeholders, what are called norms in regime theory. Only when principles are accepted together with the accompanying norms can agreements on specific rules and procedures for implementing them be reached. In Internet governance, a consensus is beginning to emerge, after Rio, on principles and some of the norms.

The fact that the main stakeholders themselves in their respective institutions reach decisions by consensus clearly has helped. Technical groups like the IETF and the W3C use "rough consensus" to adopt standards. The civil society caucuses, using intense (and voluminous) communication over Internet list-servers also achieve common positions by consensus. And, of course, intergovernmental decision-making has almost always been by consensus. In that sense, all of the stakeholders understand how agreements are made.

An additional factor in consensus is that the starting point is always ideas and analysis. In the IGF process, the role of academics and scientists has been particularly evident. Perhaps because they write so much, but probably because they apply analytical methods, scholars like Wolfgang Kleinwächter, Bill Drake, Peng Hwa Ang, and Milton Mueller have helped shape the debate.

The IGF and its predecessors have also succeeded in engaging the private sector. This reflects, to some degree, the fact that the private sector is increasingly global and transnational rather than multinational in organization. Their business models have to take into account global developments and global policies. It also reflects a trend where the United Nations has sought to find means of engaging the private sector to solve problems, either through charitable vehicles like the Global Fund or directly through mechanisms like the Global Compact. The most active private sector participants in the IGF, like Cisco, Google, Nokia and Ericsson, clearly see that their businesses can be affected positively by agreements that establish orderly processes in the Internet, and for that reason they have an incentive to be active and direct participants over time.

The total consensus package has to be accepted by governments, the private sector and civil society if it is to work. What is remarkable here is the recognition that the agreements themselves have to be multi-stakeholder. Given that most major international agreements take decades to reach, the pace of agreement on Internet governance has been relatively rapid. This seems to have been facilitated by the very open process of discussion, reflection and negotiation. The fact that the process has been defined as "not for decision-making" has reduced some of the political constraints to moving toward a decision.

An additional positive element is the fact that the individuals involved in all of the stakeholder groups have been remarkably consistent. This in itself is not unusual, since in any area where international agreements are reached there are always a mix of veterans and new people. The constancy of involvement of individuals in the IGF and its predecessors, however, is extremely high. If the same persons come to meeting after meeting, they inevitably get to know each other. Networks are created and this facilitates agreement since not only are the different positions known, so are the reasons that they are taken. This is the kind of networking whose importance was noted by Anne Marie Slaughter in her study of international law and its implementation.[3] In each successive iteration of the IGF, the networking grows stronger.

Another factor explaining the success is the IGF secretariat. It is indeed light, underfunded and with only a few staff members. But it has developed a particularly effective mode of operation. Without appearing to, it has steered the process. Part of its success is that the staff clearly understand where the different stakeholders are coming from. The executive secretary, Markus Kummer, was himself a negotiator, so he understands the intergovernmental process. Other staff members, including short-term consultants, have come from academia, the private sector and civil society. But it is not merely a matter of who is recruited. The secretariat has consciously tried to learn from the different stakeholders and, in doing so, they can recognize when consensus is possible and when further discussions are needed.

At some point, when consensus on the principles and norms is sufficiently clear, and perhaps when a crisis affects the Internet in some way, the formal intergovernmental process will kick in and governments will try to find some vehicle to formalize governance of the Internet. Although some observers might hope for a new, innovative and as yet unknown form for this, smart money is still on a framework convention, such as that which started the process of dealing with climate change.

Still, the IGF is a new model for reaching international agreements, one that goes beyond the Westphalian model that has been dominant for most of a century. The question should be asked, is this something that is unique to the Internet and therefore a one-time phenomenon, or are there lessons that can be applied to other areas in which international agreements are needed?

Part of the answer will depend on whether there will be other issues where the substance is essentially borderless, making it impossible for states alone to provide governance and where governance will need the multi-stakeholder model found in the IGF. There is clearly an increasing number of these issue areas.

Climate change is obviously one of these and the agreements to date reflect some of the elements that have characterized the IGF. The initial factual basis for the United Nations Framework Convention on Climate Change came from an epistemic community of scientists. As the regime has evolved, that scientific community, through the Intergovernmental Panel on Climate Change (IPCC) that shared the 2007 Nobel Peace Prize, has played the role of intellectual driver. The IPCC is a network of some 2,000 scientists who reach a rough consensus on what is happening in climate change and the probable implications. Civil society is a major stakeholder, helping mobilize public opinion to influence political decision-makers. The private sector, both as a producer of "green" technology and of carbon emissions has to be a player and can be engaged because of the business model implications. And the role of international organizations and their secretariats, like the World Meteorological Organization and the Secretariat of the UN Framework Convention on Climate Change, is already evident both in organizing the amassing of facts and in facilitating consensus agreements.

As the world increasingly globalizes, we can envisage even more areas where a multi-stakeholder approach to governance would become a means to reaching agreements to deal with global problems. At some point, not very far in the future, the provision of energy, given the decline of renewable resources, will become a global issue. This has been described, in Cassandra-like terms, by James Howard Kunstler in his book *The Long Emergency*.[4] Like climate change, coping with energy will require sound public policies, but the locus of action will still be the private sector that supplies energy, develops technology to use it and applies its economic power to influence those policies. In the end, the public, influenced by civil society organizations, will have to both accept behavioral changes and elect leaders who will create and implement difficult public policy choices. Like climate change and Internet governance, there is no natural international organization to deal with the issue in a comprehensive sense, although the IAEA covers the nuclear energy part and the issues of energy are bound up with other regimes.

So, if the multi-stakeholder approach to solving problems of Internet governance is the frontier of international institutions today, it may, within a reasonable time period, become the main method. If so, much of international relations theory, based on realist models, will have to be reviewed. As a minimum, the experience of the Internet governance process and the tools used to analyze it, can be applied to other areas both to understand what is happening and to help make further progress.

Notes

Foreword

1 UNDP, *Human Development Report 2001: Making New Technologies Work for Human Development* (New York: Oxford University Press, 2001), 6.
2 Craig N. Murphy, *International Organization and Industrial Change: Global Governance since 1850* (Cambridge: Polity, 1994), Emphasis in original.
3 The term "information superhighway" was reputedly first coined by Nam June Paik in 1974 in a study he wrote for the Rockefeller Foundation. It was later popularized by U.S. vice-president Al Gore.
4 John Mathiason, *Invisible Governance. International Secretariats in World Politics* (Bloomfield, Conn.: Kumerian Press, 2007).

Introduction

1 The statement is quoted by Ryan Singel, Luke O'Brien, and Kevin Poulsen on their Wired Blog 27B Stroke 6 of 30 June 2006 (http://blog.wired.com/27bstroke6/2006/06/your_own_person.html).
2 There is no formal definition for when the Internet began, but one agreed starting point is 1 January 1983 when the ARPANET converted to the TCP/IP, which is the protocol that currently makes the Internet work. See Barry M. Leiner, Vinton G. Cerf, David D. Clark, Robert E. Kahn, Leonard Kleinrock, Daniel C. Lynch, Jon Postel, Larry G. Roberts, and Stephen Wolff, *A Brief History of the Internet*, Reston, Va: Internet Society version 3.32, last revised 10 December 2003 (www.isoc.org/internet/history/brief.shtml).
3 T. Rutkowski, "The Internet Is Its Own Revolution," *Internet Society News* 2, no. 3 (autumn 1993): 2.
4 Don McLean, ed., *Internet Governance: A Grand Collaboration* (New York: United Nations ICT Task Force, 2005).
5 John R. Mathiason and Charles Kuhlman, "International Public Regulation of the Internet: Who Will Give You Your Domain Name?," Paper delivered at the annual Convention of the International Studies Association, Minneapolis, 21 March 1998; and John Mathiason and Charles Kuhlman, "An International Communication Policy: The Internet, International Regulation and New Policy Structures," paper presented at the annual convention of the International Telecommunications Society, Stockholm, Sweden, June 1998.

6 Milton Mueller, *Ruling the Root: Internet Governance and the Taming of Cyberspace* (Cambridge, Mass.: MIT Press, 2002).
7 John Mathiason, Milton Mueller, Hans Klein, Marc Holitscher, and Lee McKnight, *Internet Governance: The State of Play*, Internet Governance Project, 9 September 2004, www.internetgovernance.org/pdf/ig-sop-final.pdf).
8 See the full list at www.internetgovernance.org/index.html

1 What is the Internet and what is governance?

1 The discussion of the differences between traditional telephony and the Internet is based on the paper prepared by John Mathiason and Charles Kuhlman, "An International Communication Policy: The Internet, International Regulation and New Policy Structures," presented at the annual convention of the International Telecommunications Society, Stockholm, Sweden, June 1998. The comparison used here was prepared by Kuhlman who was, at the time, director of telecommunications at New York University.
2 This illustration and the next are taken from Vint Cerf's Powerpoint presentation entitled "Internet 101" to the United Nations ICT Task Force Global Forum on Internet Governance, New York, 24–26 March 2004, www.unicttaskforce.org/perl/documents.pl?id=1330
3 Milton Mueller, John Mathiason, and Hans Klein, "The Internet and Global Governance: Principles and Norms for a New Regime," *Global Governance* 13, no. 2 (2007): 244.
4 Don McLean, "Herding Schrödinger's Cats: Some Conceptual Tools for Thinking about Internet Governance," in Don Maclean, ed., *Internet Governance: A Grand Collaboration* (New York: UN ICT Task Force, 2004), 79–80.
5 Stephen D. Krasner, "Structural Causes and Regime Consequences: Regimes as Intervening Variables," *International Organization* 32, no. 2 (1982): 186.
6 Krasner, "Structural Causes and Regime Consequences," 186.
7 John Mathiason, Milton Mueller, Hans Klein, and Lee McKnight, "Internet Governance: The State of Play," paper prepared for the United Nations Information and Communication Technologies Task Force, 10 September 2004, www.unicttaskforce.org/perl/documents.pl?id=1389.
8 Geneva Plan of Action, paragraph 13(b)(i).
9 Tunis Agenda, paragraph 34.
10 Working Group on Internet Governance, *Report of the Working Group on Internet Governance*, World Summit on the Information Society document WSIS-II/PC-3/DOC/5-E, 3 August 2005, paras. 15–28.
11 Bruce Sterling, *The Hacker Crackdown: Law and Disorder on the Electronic Frontier* (New York: Bantam, 1993), 136.

2 Before the Internet

1 The historical information, unless otherwise noted, is drawn from International Telecommunications Union, *About the ITU: History*, www.itu.int/aboutitu/overview/history.html
2 Convention télégraphique internationale conclue à Paris, le 17 mai 1865, (parties included France, Austria, the Grand Duchy of Baden, Bavaria, Belgium, Denmark, Spain, Greece, Hanover, the Free City of Hamburg,

Italy, the Netherlands, Portugal, Prussia, Russia, the Kingdom of Saxony, Sweden and Norway, Switzerland, Turkey, and Wurtemburg).

3 This process is analyzed in Craig Murphy, *International Organization and Industrial Change: Global Governance since 1850* (New York: Oxford University Press, 1994).

4 This is well described in Peter F. Cowhey, "The International Telecommunications Regime: The Political Roots of Regimes for High Technology," *International Organization* 44, no. 2 (1990): 169–99.

5 In 1992, when Carl Malamud was working as a consultant for the ITU on the Internet, he noted that the telephones in ITU headquarters were all models whose technology dated to World War II. He took that as a symptom that the organization was hopelessly behind the times at the dawn of the digital age. See Carl Malamud, *Exploring the Internet: A Technical Travelogue* (New York: Prentice-Hall, 1992).

6 The full text of Article 19 of the International Covenant on Civil and Political Rights reads:

1 Everyone shall have the right to hold opinions without interference.

2 Everyone shall have the right to freedom of expression; this right shall include freedom to seek, receive and impart information and ideas of all kinds, regardless of frontiers, either orally, in writing or in print, in the form of art, or through any other media of his choice.

3 The exercise of the rights provided for in paragraph 2 of this article carries with it special duties and responsibilities. It may therefore be subject to certain restrictions, but these shall only be such as are provided by law and are necessary:
  (a) For respect of the rights or reputations of others;
  (b) For the protection of national security or of public order (ordre public), or of public health or morals.

7 Christopher May, *The World Intellectual Property Organization: Resurgence and the Development Agenda* (London: Routledge, 2007), 4. The discussion in this section draws heavily on May's analysis in his chapters 1 and 2.

8 Ibid., 7.

9 Ibid., 21–22.

10 The Supreme Court stated:

An explanation of our rejection of respondents' unprecedented attempt to impose copyright liability upon the distributors of copying equipment requires a quite detailed recitation of the findings of the District Court. In summary, those findings reveal that the average member of the public uses a VTR principally to record a program he cannot view as it is being televised and then to watch it once at a later time. This practice, known as "time-shifting," enlarges the television viewing audience. For that reason, a significant amount of television programming may be used in this manner without objection from the owners of the copyrights on the programs. For the same reason, even the two respondents in this case, who do assert objections to time-shifting in this litigation, were unable to prove that the practice has impaired the commercial value of their copyrights or has created any likelihood of future harm. Given these findings, there is no basis in the Copyright Act upon which respondents can hold petitioners liable for distributing VTR's to the general public. The Court of Appeals' holding that respondents are entitled to enjoin the distribution of VTR's, to collect royalties on the sale of such equipment, or to obtain other relief, if affirmed, would enlarge the scope of respondents' statutory monopolies to encompass control over an article of commerce that is not the subject of copyright protection. Such an expansion of the copyright privilege is beyond the limits of the grants authorized by Congress.

(464 U.S. 417, 104 S. Ct. 774, 78 L. Ed. 2d 574 (1984))

11 World Trade Organization, "Intellectual Property: Protection and Enforcement," *Understanding the WTO: The Agreements*, www.wto.org/english/thewto_e/whatis_e/tif_e/agrm7_e.htm

3 The non-state actors

1 Barry M. Leiner, Vinton G. Cerf, David D. Clark, Robert E. Kahn, Leonard Kleinrock, Daniel C. Lynch, Jon Postel, Larry G. Roberts, and Stephen Wolff, *A Brief History of the Internet*, Internet Society (an online document found at www.isoc.org/internet/history/brief.shtml). The next three paragraphs draw on that history.
2 The information for this description is taken from S. Bradner, "The Internet Standards Process—Revision 3," Network Working Group, Request for Comments: 2026 BCP: 9, October 1996 (ftp://ftp.isi.edu/in-notes/rfc2026.txt).
3 Bradner, "The Internet Standards Process—Revision 3," 12.
4 Internet Engineering Task Force, *Overview of the IETF*, www.ietf.org/overview.html
5 International Electro-Technical Commission, *About the IEC*, www.iec.ch/about/mission-e.htm
6 This paragraph is drawn from Tim Berners-Lee's original proposal, "Information Management: A Proposal," March 1989, May 1990, www.w3.org/History/1989/proposal.html
7 World Wide Web Consortium, *Overview*, www.w3.org/Consortium/Overview.html#mission
8 Ibid.
9 World Wide Web Consortium, *Process Document*, www.w3.org/2005/10/Process-20051014/intro.html#Intro
10 World Wide Web Consortium, *History*, www.w3.org/Consortium/history
11 www.usdoj.gov/atr/cases/f3800/msjudgex.htm#findings
12 Microsoft vs. Commission of the European Communities, http://curia.europa.eu/jurisp/cgi-bin/form.pl?lang=EN&Submit=rechercher&numaff=T-201/04
13 "Microsoft Ruling May Bode Ill for Other Companies," *New York Times*, 18 September 2007.
14 W. Russell Neuman, Lee McKnight, and Richard Jay Solomon, *The Gordian Knot: Political Gridlock on the Information Highway* (Cambridge, Mass.: MIT Press, 1997).
15 Michael Hauben and Rhonda Hauben, *Netizens: On the History and Impact of Usenet and the Internet* (New York: Wiley-IEEE Computer Society Press, 1997), x–xi.
16 http://en.wikipedia.org/wiki/Usenet

17 Hauben and Hauben, *Netizens*, 319.
18 This section is largely drawn from Bruce Sterling, *The Hacker Crackdown: Law and Disorder on the Electronic Frontier* (New York: Bantam, 1993).
19 John Perry Barlow, "Crime and Puzzlement," www.totse.com/en/technology/cyberspace_the_new_frontier/barlow.html
20 Electronic Frontier Foundation, "A History of Protecting Freedom Where Law and Technology Collide," www.eff.org/about/history.php
21 Computer Professionals for Social Responsibility, "CPSR History," www.cpsr.org/about/history
22 Association for Progressive Communication, *Annual Report 2000*, www.apc.org/english/about/history/apc_ar_2000.pdf
23 Association for Progressive Communications, *About*, www.apc.org/english/about/index.shtml

4 Solving the domain name problem

1 Milton Mueller, *Ruling the Root: Internet Governance and the Taming of Cyberspace* (Cambridge, Mass.: MIT Press, 2002), 1. Mueller's book is the most thorough study of the origins of ICANN, as well as its early development. I have drawn on it extensively for this analysis.
2 The discussion here is largely taken from Charles Kuhlman's and my 1998 study of the domain name controversy that was presented in two papers, neither of which was published, although they have been quoted extensively. It was first given to the International Studies Association 1999 Convention, but not published (John R. Mathiason and Charles C. Kuhlman, "International Public Regulation of the Internet: Who Will Give You Your Domain Name?" Paper presented to the Panel on Cyberhype or the Deterritorialization of Politics? The Internet in a Post-Westphalian Order, International Studies Association, Minneapolis, 21 March 1998. Available at www.intlmgt.com/domain.html).
3 John R. Mathiason and Charles C. Kuhlman, "An International Communication Policy: The Internet, International Regulation and New Policy Structures," paper presented at the International Telecommunications Society Convention, Stockholm, Sweden, 1998, and available at www.un.org/esa/socdev/enable/access2000/ITSpaper.html
4 United States District Court Central District of California, Lockheed Martin Corporation, Plaintiff, vs. Network Solutions, Inc., and DOES 1–20, Defendants. Case No. CV 96–7438 DDP (ANx) http://lw.bna.com/lw/19971209/967438.htm
5 Table 1 of Mathiason and Kuhlman, "International Public Regulation of the Internet," 1998, 10.
6 Table 3 from ibid., 15.
7 Table 4 from ibid., 17.
8 United States Department of Commerce, *Management of Internet Names and Addresses*, docket number 980212036-8146-02, 5 June 1998 (www.ntia.doc.gov/ntiahome/domainname/6_5_98dns.htm).
9 Ibid.

5 Regulatory imperatives for Internet governance

1 *ZDNET News*, "'Pokey' retains right to cartoon domain name," 21 April 1998, http://news.zdnet.com/2100-9595_22-509157.html

2 Statistics from WIPO, Domain Resolution Statistics, www.wipo.int/amc/en/ domains/statistics/ as of 15 October 2007. The process is described by WIPO in these terms: "Under the standard dispute clause of the Terms and Conditions for the registration of a gTLD domain name, the registrant must submit to such proceedings."

The UDRP permits complainants to file a case with a resolution service provider, specifying, mainly, the domain name in question, the respondent or holder of the domain name, the registrar with whom the domain name was registered and the grounds for the complaint. Such grounds include, as their central criteria, the way in which the domain name is identical or similar to a trademark to which the complainant has rights; why the respondent should be considered as having no rights or legitimate interests in respect of the domain name that is the subject of the complaint; and why the domain name should be considered as having been registered and used in bad faith.

The respondent is offered the opportunity to defend itself against the allegations. The provider (e.g.: the WIPO Arbitration and Mediation Center) appoints a panelist who decides whether or not the domain(s) should be transferred.

(www.wipo.int/amc/en/center/faq/domains.html#8)

3 May, *The World Intellectual Property Organization*, chapter 6.
4 Wikipedia, Sony Corp. of America vs. Universal City Studios, Inc., citing 464 U.S. 417 (1984), http://en.wikipedia.org/wiki/Sony_Corp._v._Universal_City_Studios
5 Amy Harmon, "Music Industry in Global Fight on Web Copies," *New York Times*, 7 October 2002.
6 Matt Schruers and Jonathan Band, "*Universal Music Australia Pty Ltd. v. Sharman License Holdings Ltd.*, [2005] FCA 1242," www.policybandwidth.com/doc/SharmanFinal.pdf
7 Sam Costello, "Russian Programmer Sklyarov Pleads Not Guilty, Protests Continue," *InfoWorld*, 30 August 2001, www.infoworld.com/articles/hn/xml/01/08/30/010830hnrussian.html
8 These issues are discussed extensively in Lawrence Lessig, *Free Culture: How Big Media Uses Technology and the Law to Lock Down Culture and Control Creativity* (New York: The Penguin Press, 2004), especially in chapter 10.
9 Steve Jobs, "Thoughts on Music," www.apple.com/hotnews/thoughtsonmusic/ 6 February 2007.
10 This is discussed, with links to the songs, in http://ccnmtl.columbia.edu/projects/law/library/cases/case_fantfogerty.html
11 IP Justice, *About*, http://ipjustice.org/wp/about/mission/
12 BBC News, "Call to Regulate the Net Rejected," 29 August 2007 (http://news.bbc.co.uk/go/pr/fr/-/2/hi/technology/6968322.stm).
13 ITWeek, "Estonia under Cyber-Attack," 17 May 2007 (www.itweek.co.uk/vnunet/news/2190172/estonia-under-cyberattack).
14 Council of Europe, Convention on Cybercrime, Budapest, 23 November 2001, http://conventions.coe.int/Treaty/EN/Treaties/Html/185.htm
15 International Telecommunications Union, *Final Acts of the Plenipotentiary Conference (Antalya, 2006)*, Resolution 130 (Rev. Antalya, 2006), www.itu.int/ITU-D/cyb/cybersecurity/docs/security-related-extracts-pp-06.pdf

6 The ICANN experiment

1 Internet Corporation for Assigned Names and Numbers, *Draft ICANN Strategic Plan July 2008 – June 2011*, www.icann.org/strategic-plan/draft_stratplan_2008_2011_clean_en_v1.pdf

2 United States Department of Commerce, *Management of Internet Names and Addresses*, docket number: 980212036-8146-02, 5 June 1998, www.ntia.doc.gov/ntiahome/domainname/6_5_98dns.htm

3 International Organization for Standards, *Discover ISO*, www.iso.org/iso/about/discover-iso_meet-iso/discover-iso_why-standards-matter.htm

4 Milton Mueller, *Ruling the Root: Internet Governance and the Taming of Cyberspace* (Cambridge, Mass.: MIT Press, 2002), chapter 8.

5 Ibid., 176.

6 Ibid., 177.

7 Esther Dyson, "The Electronic Frontier Foundation—Esther Dyson Becomes Board Member," *RELease 1.0*, 30 June 1991.

8 Biography posted by the Internet Corporation for Assigned Names and Numbers (www.icann.org/biog/roberts.htm).

9 Anyone interested in the details of this period should consult Mueller, *Ruling the Root*, chapter 9.

10 RIPE Network Coordination Centre, www.ripe.net/

11 Internet Corporation for Assigned Names and Numbers, Domain Name Supporting Organization, *Constituency Group Formation Process*, www.icann.org/dnso/constituency_groups.html

12 Internet Corporation for Assigned Names and Numbers, Domain Names Supporting Organization, *Names Council Chairs Over Time*, www.dnso.org/dnso/notes/20020829.NCchairs-over-time.html

13 Internet Corporation for Assigned Names and Numbers, Domain Names Supporting Organization, *DNSO Names Council Teleconference on October 5th, 1999—results*, www.dnso.org/dnso/notes/19991005.NCtelecon-minutes.html

14 Internet Corporation for Assigned Names and Numbers, Domain Names Supporting Organization, *"Convention-Style Voting Procedure" by Andrew McLaughlin*, mclaughlin@pobox.com, 23 September 1999, www.dnso.org/dnso/notes/conventionstyle.html

15 Mueller, *Ruling the Root*, 198–201.

16 Hans Klein, "The Feasibility of Global Democracy: Understanding ICANN's At-large Election," *info* 3, no. 4 (August 2001): 342. Klein later became one of the founding partners of the Internet Governance Project.

17 Martyn Williams, "ICANN Announces At-large Election Results," *NetworkWorld*, 10 October 2000. www.networkworld.com/news/2000/1011icannelect.html

18 Klein, "The Feasibility of Global Democracy," 334.

19 Ibid., 345.

20 ICANN, *Review of the Nominating Committee, 24 October 2007*, www.icann.org/reviews/nomcom-28feb07.htm

21 ICANN, Governmental Advisory Committee, *Operating Principles, 25 May 1999, Principle 1*, http://gac.icann.org/web/docs/Operating_Principles-English.htm

22 ICANN, *The Bylaws of the ICANN GNSO Noncommercial Users Constituency (Version 2.1, Approved August 2003)*, www.ncdnhc.org/current_charter.htm

23 ICANN, *Whois Services*, www.icann.org/topics/whois-services/
24 ICANN, *Staff Overview of Recent GNSO WHOIS Activities, 11 October 2007*, 3. http://gnso.icann.org/drafts/icann-staff-overview-of-whois11oct07.pdf
25 IANA, *Top Level Domains*, www.iana.org/gtld/gtld.htm
26 ICANN, Governmental Advisory Committee, *GAC Communiqué*, Wellington, New Zealand, 28 March 2006, http://gac.icann.org/web/communiques/gac24com.pdf
27 "Worldwide but Homegrown," *New York Times*, 30 October 2005.
28 Milton Mueller, "Triple X, Internet Content Regulation and the ICANN Regime," Internet Governance Project, 16 January 2007, www.internetgovernance.org/pdf/new-xxx-contract.pdf

7 Multi-stakeholderism emerges from the World Summit on the Information Society

1 Michael Schechter, *United Nations Global Conferences* (London: Routledge, 2005).
2 International Telecommunications Union, *Plenipotentiary 98—A New Beginning for the ITU?* www.itu.int/newsarchive/press/PP98/Documents/Backgrounder1_General.html
3 Ibid.
4 www.itu.int/wsis/basic/background.html
5 The agreement, however, was not reported in the 1999 annual report of the CEB. Utsumi briefed his fellow executive heads of UN system organizations, who expressed support, as they almost always do.
6 United Nations, *Report of the Economic and Social Council for 2000* (A/55/3/Rev.1), para. 12.
7 Ibid., para. 17 (10).
8 United Nations System, Administrative Committee on Coordination, *Summary of the Conclusions of the Administrative Committee on Coordination at Its Second Regular Session of 2000* (ACC/2000/20), para. 42.
9 WSIS Executive Secretariat, "Compilation of Statements Made at PREPCOM-1 on Themes and Content of the World Summit on the Information Society (WSIS)," Reference Document 1-E, 13 August 2002.
10 Outcome of the informal meeting of subcommittee 2 of PrepCom I of the WSIS, 18 September 2002.
11 Civil Society Coordination Group, document WSIS/PC-2/CONTR/71-E 5 February 2003, www.itu.int/dms pub/itu-s/md/03/wsispc2/c/S03-WSISPC2-C-0071!!PDF-E.pdf
12 "Report of the Second Meeting of the Preparatory Committee," Document WSIS/PC-2/12 (Rev.1)-E, 28 February 2003.
13 "Draft Action Plan Based on Discussions in the Working Group of Sub-Committee 2," Document WSIS/PC-2/DT/3-E 27 February 2003, www.itu.int/dms_pub/itu-s/md/03/wsispc2/td/030217/S03-WSISPC2-030217-TD-GEN-0003!!PDF-E.pdf
14 "Final Report of the Resumed Sessions of the Third Meeting of the Preparatory Committee," Document WSIS/PC-3/DOC/15-E, 27 April 2004, www.itu.int/dms_pub/itu-s/md/03/wsispc3/doc/S03-WSISPC3-DOC-0015!!PDF-E.pdf
15 WSIS Civil Society Plenary, "Shaping Information Societies for Human Needs," Civil Society Declaration to the World Summit on the Information

Society, 8 December 2003, www.itu.int/wsis/docs/geneva/civil-society-declara tion.pdf
16 Don Maclean, "Herding Schrödinger's Cats: Some Conceptual Tools for Thinking about Internet Governance," background paper for the ITU Workshop on Internet Governance, Geneva, 26–27 February 2004, www. itu.int/osg/spu/forum/intgov04/contributions/itu-workshop-feb-04-internet-governance-background.pdf
17 www.unicttaskforce.org/perl/documents.pl?id=1389
18 JUSCANZ consists of Japan, the United States, Canada, Australia, and New Zealand.
19 www.wgig.org/docs/chairman-summary.pdf
20 Peng Hwa Ang, *Ordering Chaos: Regulating the Internet* (Singapore: Thomson, 2005).
21 www.wgig.org/docs/ChairIntroPrepCom.pdf
22 www.itu.int/wsis/docs2/pc2/off5.pdf
23 www.wgig.org/docs/IG-questionnaire-response.pdf
24 www.chathamhouse.org.uk/about/chathamhouserule/
25 Nitin Desai, "Preface," in *Reforming Internet Governance: Perspectives from the Working Group on Internet Governance (WGIG)*, ed. William Drake (New York: United Nations Information and Communication Technology Task Force, 2005), ix–x.
26 www.wgig.org/docs/WGIGREPORT.pdf
27 www.itu.int/wsis/docs2/pc3/working/dt7rev2.pdf
28 www.itu.int/wsis/docs2/pc3/working/dt15.pdf
29 www.itu.int/wsis/docs2/tunis/off/6rev1.pdf

8 The IGF experiment begins

1 Internet Governance Forum, "Consultations on the Convening of the Internet Governance Forum Transcript of Afternoon Session 17 February 2006," www.intgovforum.org/contributions/UN-IGF-PM-2-17-06.txt
2 Internet Governance Forum, Short synthesis of written contributions and discussions, www.intgovforum.org/brief.htm
3 Internet Governance Forum, "Summing Up Session Transcript, 1 November 2006," www.intgovforum.org/IGF-Summing_Up_Nov_1.txt
4 John Mathiason and Charles Kuhlman, "International Public Regulation of the Internet: Who Will Give You Your Domain Name?" Paper presented to the panel on "Cyberhype or the Deterritorialization of Politics? The Internet in a Post-Westphalian Order," International Studies Association Convention, Minneapolis, Minn., 21 March 1998, pp. 27–29.
5 John Mathiason, "A Framework Convention: An Institutional Option for Internet Governance," a Concept Paper by the Internet Governance Project, December 2004 (www.internetgovernance.org/pdf/igp-fc.pdf).
6 Internet Governance Forum, Workshop Report, 1. Title: "Exploring a Framework Convention on the Internet," www.intgovforum.org/Athens_workshops/Framework%20convention%20workshop%20Report.pdf
7 IGF Secretariat, "Summing Up of the Inaugural Session of the Internet Governance Forum, Athens, 30 October–2 November 2006," www.intgov forum.org/Summary.Final.07.11.2006.htm

8 John Mathiason, *The Road to Rio and Beyond: Results-Based Management of the UN Internet Governance Forum*, Internet Governance Project, 23 October 2006 (www.internetgovernance.org/pdf/roadtorio.pdf)

9 Internet Governance Forum, "Internet Governance Forum Consultations Wednesday 23 May 2007 10:00 a.m.," www.intgovforum.org/May_contribu tions/IGF-23May07Consultation.txt

10 Internet Governance Forum, "Dynamic Coalitions," http://intgovforum. org/dynamic_coalitions.php?listy=4

11 Internet Bill of Rights Dynamic Coalition, "Report from the Conference 'Dialogue Forum on Internet Rights—Italy 2007,'" www.internet-bill-of-rights.org/en/report_20070927.php

12 Milton Mueller, "Net Neutrality as Global Principle for Internet Governance," Internet Governance Project, 5 November 2007 (www.internet governance.org/pdf/NetNeutralityGlobalPrinciple.pdf).

13 The quotes from the Critical Internet Resources session are taken from the transcript at http://intgovforum.org/Rio_Meeting/IGF2-Critical%20Internet %20Resources-12NOV07.txt

14 Internet Governance Forum, "Second Meeting of the Internet Governance Forum (IGF), Rio de Janeiro, 12–15 November 2007, Chairman's Summary," http://intgovforum.org/Rio_Meeting/Chairman%20Summary. FINAL.16.11.2007.pdf

15 Internet Governance Forum, "Internet Governance Forum 2 Rio de Janeiro 15 November 2007 Emerging issues," http://intgovforum.org/Rio_Meeting/ IGF2-EmergingIssues-15NOV07.txt

16 Internet Governance Forum, "Internet Governance Forum 2 Rio de Janeiro, Brazil 15 November 2007 Closing ceremony," http://intgovforum. org/Rio_Meeting/IGF2-Closing-15NOV07.txt

17 Personal interview with Jeanette Hofmann, Rio de Janeiro, 15 November 2007.

9   What does the frontier look like?

1 Geoffrey Allen Pigman, *The World Economic Forum: A Multi-Stakeholder Approach to Global Governance* (London: Routledge, 2006).

2 Peter M. Haas, "Introduction: Epistemic Communities and International Policy Coordination," *International Organization* 46, no. 1 (1992): 1–35.

3 Anne Marie Slaughter, *A New World Order* (Princeton, N.J.: Princeton University Press, 2005).

4 James Howard Kunstler, *The Long Emergency: Surviving the End of Oil, Climate Change, and Other Converging Catastrophes of the Twenty-First Century* (New York: Atlantic Monthly Press, 2005).

Select bibliography

Peng Hwa Ang, *Ordering Chaos: Regulating the Internet* (Singapore: Thomson, 2005). A Third-World perspective on what Internet governance means.

William L. Drake, ed., *Reforming Internet Governance: Perspectives from the Working Group on Internet Governance (WGIG)* (New York: UN ICT Task Force Series 12, 2005). A collective memoir of the work of the working group that set the stage for the Internet Governance Forum.

Lawrence Lessig, *The Future of Ideas: The Fate of the Commons in a Connected World* (New York: Vintage Books, 2002). A thorough discussion about problems with intellectual property in the Internet Age.

Christopher May, *The World Intellectual Property Organization: Resurgence and the Development Agenda* (London and New York: Routledge, 2006). A thorough but readable study of one of the formal international organizations that is concerned with Internet governance.

Don McLean, ed., *Internet Governance: A Grand Collaboration* (New York: United Nations, 2005). A compilation of thoughtful essays that was very influential in shaping the issue.

Milton Mueller, *Ruling the Root: Internet Governance and the Taming of Cyberspace* (Cambridge, Mass.: MIT Press, 2004). A study of the early, and somewhat tempestuous period of the Internet Corporation for Assigned Names and Numbers.

Milton Mueller, John Mathiason, and Hans Klein, "The Internet and Global Governance: Principles and Norms for a New Regime," *Global Governance* 13, no. 2 (April-June 2007): 237–54. An exploration of the theoretical issues.

Andrew L. Shapiro, *The Control Revolution: How the Internet is Putting Individuals in Charge and Changing the World We Know* (New York: Public Affairs, 1999). A very early exploration of whether the Internet can be governed.

Index

N.B. Figures in **bold** type indicate a figure or a table.

Abramatic, Jean-François (chair of W3C) 77
academics, well represented at Rio (2007) 139
access, ISPs and 14; issue constrained by critical Internet resources related to IPv6 143
Address Supporting organization *see* ASO
addresses of packets, replaceable by alphabetic equivalents stored on DNS server file 9
addressing system, first governance issue of the Internet 7
adult content industry (.xxx), controversy about top-level domain name 92, 95
Advisory Board (AB) 40, 1549
Afonso, Carlos 141
African Civil Society 116
AfriNIC 78, 81
Agrawala, Pankaj (India) 134
agreement, can only be reached by consensus 147
agreement about international responsibility, cybersecurity and crime 68
Aguiar, Plínio de 140, 142
Ahon, Erick Irarte 134
Aina, Alain 140
Aizu, Izumi 79, 113
Alcatel-Lucent 139
Ali, Ben (president of Tunisia), focus on ICT 98

alphabetic names, divided into domains 9
Alternex/IBASE (Brazil) 47
America On-line, libel action against 15
American Civil Liberties Union 91
Ang, Peng Hwa 148; *Ordering Chaos: Regulating the Internet* 118, 159n20
Annan, Kofi (UN Secretary-General) 109
anonymizers (hide the source of transmission) 67
APC 47–48, 91, 127, 137, 139–40, 155n22; ICANN and 105, 107; Karen Banks and 115–16, 132
APNIC (Asia and the Pacific), Pindar Wong 78
Apple, monopoly in downloadable music 40, 42–43, 64
Apple iTunes, fees to copyright holders included in cost of download DRM 62
area codes, denote geographic place with identifiable boundaries 9
ARIN (North and South America), Ken Fockler 78
ARPANET 32, 43
Article 19 27, 153n6
ASO, converted DNSO into two different organizations 83; regional Internet registries 77–78, 82–83, 157n10

Association for Progressive
Communication *see* APC
AT&T long-distance switching system,
major crash (15 January 1990) 45
At-Large Advisory Committee
(ALAC) 82–83
"at-large council" 80
at-large members, elections 79–80
Athens forum, (2006) structure **132**,
139; avoided critical Internet
resources 140; concept of dynamic
coalitions somewhat vague 137;
euphoria about 135; (November
2006) 3, 126, 129; themes of
Openness, Access, Diversity and
Security 136; workshop
"Exploring a Framework
Convention on the Internet" 133
Auerbach, Karl 79–80, 113
Australia 130
Australia and New Zealand,
broadcasting as a public service 29
Austria, shut down ISP by
confiscating its physical servers
15
"bandwidth", speed with which
packets can be sent 11
bandwidth, finite resource, ITU set
up procedure to allocate
frequencies 26

Banks, Karen 115–16, 132
Barlow, John Perry 45; essay "Crime
and Puzzlement" 46
Bell System-affiliated companies,
evolution of US ten-digit area
code-exchange-line number system
9
BellSouth telephone company,
hacker in Georgia (1989) 45
Berkman Center at Harvard
University, Names Council
teleconference (October 1999) 78
Berne Convention for the Protection
of Literary and Artistic Works
(Paris 1871) 28–29; Article 10 (2)
29–30
Berners-Lee, Tim 37–38, 154n6
Betamax or other VCRs, not liable
for infringement 61–62, 156n4

bilateral and regional agreements,
standardize telegraph equipment
24, 152n1
"bots", definition 67–68
Box 1.1, Policy issues that needed to
be addressed in Internet
governance 19
Box 6.1, Generic top-level domain
names (October 2007) 94–95
Brazil 104, 117, 120–22, 129,
136–37, 140
Brazilian minister of science and
technology, Rio conference (2007)
140
Brief history of the Internet 154n1
browser 38
Budweiser beer, trademarked in
United States and other countries
by Anheuser Busch 60
Bureau of PrepCom, observers and
107, 109
Bureau of WSIS, open-ended
intergovernmental drafting group
106
Bureaux Internationaux Réunis pour
la Protection de la Propriété
Intellectuelle (BIRPPI) 29
Bush administration, unilateral
action and involvement in Iraq
96

Cabell, Diane 79
Campos, Ivan Moura 81
Canada 9; representative from 137
Caribbean 9, 120
CEB, satisfied with draft plan and
stressed early decision by ITU 100
Cerf, Vinton 32, 65–66, 77, 84–85,
99, 115, 140–43, 158n6
CERN 37–38, 116
"chairman's food for thought paper"
124
Chango, Mawaki (African Civil
Society) 91
channel or medium 6–7, 12–13, 15
Chapelle, Bertrand de la 113, 115,
134
Chatham House Rule 121
child pornography, universal
agreement this is prohibited 66–67

Chile 136
China 120, 132, 136; effort to have
    search engines block certain sites
    65, 133; entry to WTO delayed till
    it agreed to crack down on pirated
    software 62
China (.cn) 89
China Internet Network Information
    Center 34
Cisco Systems 34, 36, 127, 132, 139,
    148
civil liberties groups 76
civil sector, role in the Internet 2
civil society 18, 112–13, 149
Civil Society Caucus 23,137
civil society caucuses, achieve
    common positions by consensus 147
Civil Society Coordination Group,
    NGOs and 105
Civil Society Internet Forum (CSIF)
    80
Cleveland Free-Net, experiment in
    publicly available network 44
climate change, agreement that
    reflects elements of IGF 149
Clinton, Hillary Rodham 54
Cohen, Jonathan 79
commercial interests, scramble for
    cyberspace xiv
Committee for a Democratic United
    Nations 137
Committee on ICANN Evolution
    and Reform 82
Committee on Restructuring 82
common domain names, only one
    register for the five (1998) 50,
    155n2
Communications Decency Law,
    invalidation by Supreme Court in
    United States 14–15
communication, state-run enterprise 25
communication content, regulated
    by three different regimes 27
communication theory,
    communication consists of five
    parts 6
communications, international
    regulation 24
communications policy, regulatory
    policy 14

competition 56
compromise, collect fees at sender
    end and share with service that
    provided message 25
Computer Fraud and Abuse Act
    (1986) 45
Computer Liberty Foundation 46
computer makers, fought to protect
    their intellectual property 40
Computer Professionals for Social
    Responsibility (CPSR) 23, 47, 91,
    105
computers, store information in
    binary numbers (1 or 0) 7
Computers, Freedom and Privacy
    47, 155n21
Conference of NGOs 23;
    consultative relationship with the
    United Nations (CONGO) 100,
    127
consensus package, has to be
    accepted by governments, private
    sector and civil society 148
Conservative Party, ideas to curb
    access of British youth to sites like
    YouTube 65, 156n12
content, no agreement where liability
    for rests 68
content providers, the Internet and
    concern with intellectual property
    43
contentious issues 129, 159n2
Convention on Cybercrime, adopted
    by Council of Europe 68, 156n13
"convention-style voting" 79,
    157n14
convergence, questions about 141,
    160n13
copyright 28, 61–62, 64–65
cost, degree of competition among
    senders, WTO and 14
Council of Europe 139
Council of Registrars (CORE) 52,
    55
Country Code names Supporting
    Organization (ccNSO) 82
country-code domain names (cc-tlds)
    92
country-code registrars, not
    dependent on ICANN 92

court cases, trademark infringement and 51, 155n4
Covenant on Civil and Political Rights, Human Rights Committee 28
Cowley, Lesley 140
Crew, Greg 79
critical Internet resources 107, 136, 140, 143, 145
Cukier, Ken (*Economist* reporter) 132
cybercrime 46, 129
Cybercrime Convention, consists mostly of members from the Council of Europe 68
cybersecurity 129
cybersecurity and crime, international responsibility 68
"cybersquatting" 60–61
Czech Republic, Budweiser beer trademark held by *Budejovicky Budvar* 60

DARPA 32–33
Davidson, Phillip (manager for British Telecom) 77
decision-making procedures, implementing collective choice 17, 152n6
Defense Advanced Projects Administration (DARPA) 32
Dengate-Thrush, Peter 79, **85**, 88
Desai, Nitin 109, 116–17, 119, 127–29, 159n1, 159n19; closing-session summary of Rio conference 144; composition of WGIG **118**; MAG and 130; summary of closing session 134–35; WGIG book prepared by its members 121–22, 159n25
developing countries, obstacles to access providers 16
"Development and International Cooperation in the Twenty-first Century: The Role of Information Technology in the Context of a Knowledge-based Global Economy" 99
"Dialogue Forum on Internet Rights (Italy 2007) 137
Digital Millennium Copyright Act (1998) 64

digital rights management (DRM) 62, 64
digitalized content, transmitted over the Internet using standard packet-switching 62
digitalized movies, have large numbers of packets and take long time to download 11
Diplo Foundation (Geneva) 23, 116
Division for Economic and Social Council Support and Coordination 114
DNS root name servers 77
domain name controversy, internationalization of the Internet and 4, 48
domain name registrars 120
domain name registries 76, 127
Domain Name Server (1984), synonyms for digit strings of actual address 9, 56–57
Domain Name Supporting Organization (DNSO) 78, 83, 90
domain registrars, did not check if domains were trademarked by anyone 60
domain registration, problems affected order and procedures of the Internet 52
domain survey host count 2–3
Dominican Republic 103, 105–6
Doria, Avri (GNSO chair) 93, 118
"draft standard" 35
Drake, William 113, 115–16, 118–19, 134, 148
Droan, Matt and American On-Line, feedback issue 16
"dynamic coalitions" 131, 133–34, 137–38, 160n10
Dyson, Esther, on EFF 74–75, 157n7

e-mail, requires very little bandwidth 11, 38
Eastern Europe 130
Echeberria, Raul (Uruguay) 141
Economic and Social Council (ECOSOC) 99–100, 158n7
EDUCOM 74, 157n8
Egypt, offered to host 2009 forum 135

El Salvador, delegate speaking on behalf of GRULAC built case for dealing with critical Internet resources 136, 160n9
elected at-large members 79
electronic communication, spamming and phishing undermine confidence in 68
Electronic Frontier Foundation (EFF) 23, 45–47, 64–65, 74, 80
electronic media, information and xiii
Electronic Privacy Network 91
Ellis, Jim 44
email address internationalization, special problems 34
"emerging issues" 132
encryption technology, issue of 14
energy, coping with will require sound public policies 150
Ericcson 148
Esterhuyzen, Anriette (APC) 115
Estonia, web sites and servers in 68, 156n13
Ethernet Local Area Network (LAN) 11
Europe, formal arrangements to facilitate interconnection by telegraph 24; privatization of telecommunications in many countries 42
European Commission, supported by associations advocating open software 42, 154n12
European Commission scrutiny, MCI/WorldCom merger (1998) 15
European countries, multilateral agreements on copyrights 28
European Court of First instance, Microsoft had violated European competition rules 42
European organization for Nuclear Research (CERN) 37
European Union 120
Executive Committee of ICANN, members 91

factors which determine speed of packets 11
fair use 61–62, 64–65

Federal Court of Australia, *Universal Music Australia Pty Ltd. v. Sharman License Holdings Ltd.*, (2005) FCA 1242 63
feedback 12–13, 16
Figueres, Jose Maria (former president of Costa Rica) 101, 114
First descriptive sentence 119
Fockler, Ken 78
Fogerty, John (Creedence Clearwater Revival band) 65, 156n10
forum idea, support for 120–23
Foundation for Media Alternatives (Philippines) 133
Foundation for MultiMedia Communications 116
Fourth Plenipotentiary Conference of ITU (1875), United States participation 25
Fourth United Nations Conference on Women in Beijing 47, 101
Framework Convention on Internet Governance, article by John Mathiason 133, 159n5
framework of Principles 137
France 64, 116, 132
France Telecom 139
free long-distances telephone calls, individuals tried for throughout 1980s 45
Free Software Foundation of Europe 137
freedom of expression 137; government's right to block Internet content 65
frequency spectrum, borderless, considered a kind of global commons 26

GAC 82–84, 88, 157n21; change in composition 88–89; ICANN and 142; interest in how country codes allocated and managed 89–90; opposed to introduction of.xxx TLD 95, 158n26
Gage, John 99
gatekeepers including NGOs, has to be explored in channeling feedback 16

GDSO, problems with and the at-large election 83
general access 137
Generic Names Supporting Organization (GNSO) 82, 90 91, 93
generic top-level domain names (gTLDs) 50, 93
Geneva, consultation 20–21 September 2004 116; meeting 23–25 November 2004 118; Plan of Action 19, 112, 119; Preparatory Committee 1–5 July 103; Preparatory Committee 19–30 September 2005 resolved governance issues 123; PrepCom 2 (17–28 February 2003) 104–5; PrepCom 3 (10–14 November) 111; PrepCom 3 participants (3 September)109–10; summit tasks left to Tunis summit Internet governance and financing for ITCs 112; third PrepCom forced to meet November and December before summit 108
George Mason University Law Schools Critical Infrastructure Protection Program 138
German government, prosecution of CompuServe for pornographic content 14–15, 65
German Information and Communication Services Bill 14
Ghana 123
Giganet news server, 107, 127 groups (18 September 2007) 45
Global Compact 100, 148
Global Forum on Internet Governance, meeting in New York 25–26 March 2004 114
Global Fund 148
"Global governance of the Information Society should be considered" 103
Global Incorporation Alliance Workshop, later Internet Forum on the White paper (IFWP) 72
Global Information Infrastructure Commission 140
Global Internet Governance Academic Network (GIGANET) 23, 138

globalization, increasing transnational aspects of telecommunications 57, 98
GNSO, convened WHOIS Task Force (June 2005) 93
gnutella.com, P2P software 62
Good Governance 107
goods, traded across borders and tariffs applied 24
Google 65, 139, 140, 148
Gosset, Ulysse (French television program *Talk de Paris*) 140
governance, five groups of stakeholders 19, 23
governance of the Internet, new development for global governance xiv
Governmental Advisory Committee *see* GAC
governments, formalize governance when consensus on principles and norms sufficiently clear 149
Gowing, Nik (presenter of HARDtalk) 143
Greece 127, 131
"Green Paper" 54–58, 155n6
GreenNet (UK) 47
Gross, Robin (Executive Director of IP Justice) 65, 91, 130
Group of 77 120
gTLD registries, represented through ASO 78, 90
gTLD-MoU, geographical distribution of original signers 53
gTLDs 50, 93

Haas, Peter 146, 160n2
hacking 45, 68
Hamburg Chaos Computer Club 81, 157n17
Hassan, Aleysha 107, 113, 116, 118, 130
Hauben, Michael, *Netizens: On the History and Impact of Usenet and the Internet* 43–44, 154n15, 155n17
Hivos (Netherlands) 133
Hoffman, Jeanette 81, 117, 126, 130, 133, 144, 160n17
Hoffmann, Dr. Hans Falk 116

Holitscher, Marc 5
Hong Kong (.hk) 89
Hugo, Victor, copyright 28
Human Development Report (2001)
  xiv, 151n1
"hypertext" 37
"HyperText Markup language"
  (HTML) 38

IAB 32–33, **50**
IANA 50, 52, 54, 71–73, 89
IBM 139
ICANN xv, 3–4, 49, 105, 120, 127,
  130, 139; agreed on 20 tlds
  including 13 new ones 93–95,
  158n25; at-large election too
  complex 82; board of directors 76,
  83–84; bodies electing directors
  82, 157n20; by-laws and ASO 77;
  CEO at Rio (2007) 140; concern
  with country-code top-level
  domain names 88; critical Internet
  resources being developed through
  97; decisions by vote 71; directors
  to be elected by proxy voting
  78–79; dissatisfaction with the
  board and lack of transparency
  80; DNSO and 78, 157n11;
  examined by IGP colleague
  Milton Mueller 4, 152n6; funding
  and 74, 76–77, 157n9; funding for
  WGIG 116; global elections value
  of democratic governance 81–82;
  GNSO decisions passed on to
  board of 91; governance issue and
  70; governments as main
  stakeholder with limited
  involvement in 88; included
  setting up UDRP 60, 74; initial
  members of board of directors
  73–75; international organization
  71; mechanism for electing
  at-large members 79; members of
  board of directors (October 2007)
  85–88; narrow technical body at
  one level 92; not-for-profit public
  corporation in California 58,
  70–71; oversight function 121–23,
  142; pluses and minuses of xvi;
  policy activities span several areas
  18; reform process and kind of
  rough consensus 83; relationship
  with netizens 90; reluctant to
  accept issue of critical Internet
  resources 136; renegotiation of
  contract with US Department of
  Commerce 96; replacement of
  called for 113, 158–59n15;
  represents the private sector 90;
  set up to govern Internet resources
  in WSIS 69; structure of 82, **84**;
  supporting organizations 74, 77,
  83; WHOIS database 92–93,
  158n23; work to maintain cc-tld
  registries within 92; .xxx and 96
ICT 48, 68, 109
ICT for Development, agreement
  relatively easy 108
ICT Task Force, analytical papers
  *Internet Governance: A Grand
  Collaboration* 115
identification, how best to register
  domain names 12, 14
IETF 32–35, 39, 43, 73, 82–83, 120,
  130, 154n3; chairs in (September
  2007) **36**; consensus decisions 71;
  content of protocols and 12;
  ICANN 77, 92, 140; rough
  consensus 147; type of
  organization for members **37**
IGF 4, 134; compromise and 126;
  first meeting in Athens (October
  2006) 5; governance issues 145,
  147; issue of critical Internet
  resources 143; multilateral,
  multi-stakeholder, democratic and
  transparent 125; new form of
  global organization 146; new
  model for international agreements,
  goes beyond Westphalian model
  149; one of main themes for the
  future 138, 160n11; private sector
  and 148; report on web site 134,
  159n7; role of academics and
  scientists 148; secretariat to
  convene in 2006 and set out tasks
  124; transcriptions of discussions
  maintained on web site 129
IGF Athens meeting participation
  131

IGF I: Athens 131–35
IGF II: Rio 138–44
IGF III-V and beyond 144–45
IGF secretariat, convened
  stock-taking session (Geneva on
  13 February 2007) 135; effective
  mode of operation 149; no formal
  outcome document for Rio
  conference 143; took advantage of
  meetings concerning WSIS follow-
  up (Geneva May 2007) 136
IGF V, 2010 consideration to future
  of the forum 145
IMF speaker 99
India 120, 140
Indian delegate, offer to host 2008
  forum in Delhi 129
industrialized countries, wanted to
  keep intellectual property in
  WIPO and WTO 61
informal intersession, 15–18 July
  2003 in Paris 106, 109
informal meeting in Geneva from
  16–18 September 2002 103
informal meetings, way of obtaining
  text to negotiate 106
information xiv, 25, 110
Information and Communication
  Technologies Task Force (ICT-D)
  101–2, 126
Information Network 141
Information Society agenda,
  governance a core issue 111
"information superhighway" xv, 151n3
initial treaty, continental European
  countries 25, 152n3, 152–53n3
Institute of Electrical and
  Electronics Engineers Inc. (IEEE)
  37
Institute for Global Communication
  (IGC) 47
Institute of International law
  (University of Graz Austria) 137
Intel 139; monopoly in computer
  chips 40, 42
intellectual property 18, 28, 40, 43,
  49, 59–61, 64, 120
intellectual property and content
  issues, not yet discussed in depth
  145

Intellectual Property Interests 90
Intellectual Property Rights *see* IPRs
Inter-Governmental Council,
  principles of transparency and
  democracy 124, 159n28
interconnection costs 25
intergovernmental decision-making,
  consensus and 147–48
Intergovernmental Panel on Climate
  Change (IPCC) 149
intergovernmental summits, key
  events preparatory meetings 102
International Ad-Hoc Committee
  (IAHC) 52
International Atomic Energy
  Agency (IAEA) 103, 150
International Chamber of
  Commerce 100, 103, 120, 127,
  140; Ayesha Hassan and 107, 116,
  118, 130
International Committee of the Red
  Cross (Switzerland) 25
International Covenant on Civil and
  Political Rights 27–28
International Domain names in
  Application (IDNA) 33
International Electro-technical
  Commission (Geneva) 37
international governance of the
  Internet, orientation **55**
International governance issue,
  regimes and institutions affected
  by 5, 152n7
"international ('inter'-
  governmental"), placed in text
  106, 158n12
international NGOs of senders,
  composition of 14
International Organization for
  Standardization (ISO) 71, 77, 89
International Radiotelegraph
  Convention (1906) 26
international regimes, consensus
  definition of 17, 152n5
International Telegraph/
  Telecommunication Union *see*
  ITU
internationalization of the Internet,
  needs principles, norms and
  procedures 4, 151n5

Internet address space (IPV4 and
    IPv6) 77
Internet addresses, different from
    telephone numbers 9–10
Internet Architecture Board *see* IAB
Internet Assigned Numbers
    Authority *see* IANA
Internet Bill of Rights, Dynamic
    Coalition on 137
Internet Corporation for Assigned
    Names and Numbers *see* ICANN
Internet domain name and address
    system, public-private partnership
    107–8
Internet Domain Name and IP
    Address System 105
Internet Engineering Steering Group
    (IESG) 34–35
Internet Engineering Task Force *see*
    IETF
Internet Explorer, driven Netscape
    almost out of business 40
Internet Forum on the White Paper
    (IFWF) 72–73
Internet forums, web-based 44
Internet freedom movement 74
Internet governance, agreement on
    definition 122; consensus
    beginning to emerge after Rio on
    principles and norms 147;
    consensus on common text still
    outstanding 111, 158n14;
    consensus should be multilateral
    and transparent 108; multi-
    stakeholder approach to solving
    problems 150; national and
    international policy issues **13**;
    regulation of intellectual property
    turns on "fair use" 64; state and
    non-state organizations involved 18
Internet Governance Forum *see* IGF
Internet Governance Project 23, 128,
    133–34; another concept paper
    135; comment 123; institutional
    vehicle to look at the issue 5, 81,
    152n8; "Internet Governance: The
    State of Play" 115, 159n17
Internet Governance Task Force of
    Japan 120
Internet IP Postcard system 7–8

Internet issues, new issues might
    emerge with technological changes
    135, 160n8
Internet management 107, 110–11
Internet mavens, Plain Old
    Telephone Service 6
Internet Protocol (IP) 107
Internet senders and receivers, not
    tied to billing process 10
Internet service providers *see* ISPs
Internet Society 127, 139, 140; *Brief
    history of the Internet* 32;
    defended ICANN 107; IETF and
    33; NGOs 33, 55, 72, 76
Internet Society of China 120, 139
Internet Society of Ghana 81
Internet Society (ISOC)
    representative 117, 130
Internet Standard, definition 34
Internet Steering Committee of
    Brazil 140–41
Internet, the 38; 2008 38; ability of
    musicians to distribute music 65;
    addressing system is critical
    element 50; always subject to
    modicum of governance xiv;
    borderless 2–3, 7, 15, 147; can be
    "governanced" but not governed
    17; communication apparatus of
    US military xiv; concept of
    broadcasting or communication of
    content different 31; concise
    definition 11; consequences for
    telecommunications companies
    42–43; controlled by privately
    owned US company 103–4;
    designed by engineers and
    scientists for low cost data
    communication 9; downloadable
    content and intellectual property
    issues 61; free market for ideas 14;
    governments had begun to see it
    raised policy issues and 108;
    implications for pre-existing
    agreements 18; IP postcard system
    7–8; issue of freedom of
    expression in area of pornography
    66; made up of individuals who
    get services from institutions 11;
    managed from outset by civil

society 146–47; most complete
communications system yet
devised 16; most regulatory issues
still unsolved 59; network of
networks 6–7; non-state actors 32,
48; non-state actors engaged in
terrorism and 67; openness is
essential value of 65; roots xiv;
ubiquitous and powerful at
beginning of twenty-first century
2; useful for exchanging
information 37
IP Constituency 82
IP Justice 65, 137, 156n11
IP numbers of domain name servers,
entered into IANA root directory
52
IP version 6 [Ipv6] 7
IPRs xv, 28, 62, 153n7
Iran 136
ISP Constituency 82
ISPs 7, 14, 68, 90
IT for Change (Bangalore) 133
Italy 140; "Dialogue Forum on
Internet Rights" (2007) 137
ITU xv, 24, 52–53, 108, 139; (2001)
decided to set up summit in two
phases, Geneva 2003 and Tunis
2005 101; began to redefine its
identity mid-1990s when the
Internet arrived 26, 153n5; briefed
chiefs executives board about
plans for October 2001 session
101; coordinated national action
for preparation, response and
recovery of incident 69; director-
general at Rio Conference (2007)
140; expert meeting 26–27
February 2004 113–14; future
identity in question in (1998) 98,
158n2; IETF and 98;
intergovernmental forum 25;
Rutkowski and 72; secretariat
sought to become involved
through the MoU-TLD 97;
statement 68, 156n15;
telecommunications corporations
and 42; telecommunications main
channels over landlines that
passed over national borders 26;
to register the registrars 52; would
do most of the work but not be in
charge 102
ITU secretariat 25–26

Jackson, Judge Thomas Penfield,
conclusion on Microsoft case 42,
154n11
Japan 116–17, 120
Japan Broadcasting Corporation 132
Japanese Institute of Global
Communications (GLOCOM) 107
Jobs, Steve (CEO of Apple), DRM a
flawed and expensive business
model 64, 156n9
JUSCANZ 117, 159n18

Kahn, Robert 32, 113
Kapor, Mitch, spreadsheet program
Lotus 1-2-3 45–46
Karklins, Janos 84–85
Katoh, Masanobu 81
Kemna, Wolfgang 99
Khan, Sarbuland 99, 114
Klein, Hans 5, 11, 17, 80–82,
157ns16, 18–19
Klein, Norbert 91
Kleinwächter, Wolfgang 107, 113,
118, 128, 148
Kuhlman, Charles 50, 54–55
Kummer, Markus 113, 115–16, 127,
134, 149
Kunstler, James Howard, *The Long
Emergency* 150, 160n4
Kurilja, Jovan 116

Latin America 120
Latin America and Caribbean
Group of States (GRULAC) 136
law enforcement agencies, went after
owners of servers 45
Lessig, Lawrence 46, 80, 104
linguistic diversity 137
Lithuania and Azerbaijan, offered to
host 2010 forum 135
Lull, Ramon 79
Lynn, Stuart (CEO of ICANN) 82

McBride, Lee 5
McKnight, Lee 17, 43

MacLean, Don, definition of
  governance 16–17, 152n4;
  "Herding Schrödinger's Cats"
  113–15, 159n16
Madonna, appealed to WIPO
  UDRP and won 61
Madrid Conference (1932), ITU and
  26
MAG 81, 129–31, 135–37
Magaziner, Ira, appointed by
  president Clinton as Internet czar 54
Markle Foundation, funded ICANN
  election 80
Masango, Chengetai 116, 127
Massachusetts Institute of
  Technology *see* MIT
Mathiason, John 11, 17, 50, 54–55,
  134; book and xv, xvi 151n4
May, Christopher 28–29, 61, 153n9,
  156n3
Memorandum of Understanding
  with NTIA, US government
  formal oversight 58
Memorandum of Understanding on
  Top-Level Domains *see* MoU
messages 6–7, 12–14, 25
Microsoft 40, 42, 139
Millennium Summit, United
  Nations and view of ICT 99
MIT laboratory for Computer
  Science 38
Morse, Samuel F.B., invented
  telegraph 1844 24
MoU 52–53, 55, 155n5
MoUtld 60, 73, 97–98
Mueller, Milton 4–5, 11, 17, 113,
  140, 148; answer on convergence
  141; article published by Internet
  Governance Project 96, 158n28;
  chair of NCUC 91; description of
  ICANN 72, 157n4; electing at-
  large members difficult 79,
  157n15; election results
  "stunning" 80; "GAC is the
  wrong model" 142–43; IFWP 73,
  157n6; "Net Neutrality as Global
  Principle for Internet
  Governance" 138; *Ruling the Root*
  49, 155n1; on Transition Advisory
  Group 72, 157n5

Mueller-Maguhn, Andy 81
multi-stakeholder methodology,
  resolving critical Internet issues
  143, 147
multi-stakeholder process 4
multilingualism 129
Multistakeholder Advisory Group
  see MAG
Murai, Jun 74–75
Murphy, Craig xv 151n2
musicians, many do not own
  copyright of their music 65
MySpace 64–65, 133

Names Council, DNSO in Berlin
  (1999) 78
national regulation of networks,
  problems of 43, 154n14
National Science Foundation *see*
  NSF
National Telecommunications and
  Information Administration
  (NTIA) 53, 58
net addresses, neither sender nor
  receiver is paying customer for the
  packet 10
Net Dialogue Project (Harvard and
  Stanford Universities) 137
Netherlands 116, 127
netizens 43–48, 51
Netscape 11
Network Security 107
Network Solutions Inc 50–52,
  72–73, 76
Neuman, Russell 43
New Delhi, IGF III 144
New York Times 63, 96, 156n5,
  158n27
New Zealand 130; meeting (March
  2006),xxx TLD and 95
Newsgroups (Usenet groups), varied,
  changeable and chaotic 45
NGOs 65, 96, 109, 120, 127, 130,
  133, 137
Nicaragua 120
Nicarao/CRIES (Nicaragua) 47
Nigeria, spam and 67
Nokia 148
NomCom (Nominating committee)
  35, 82–84

Non-Commercial Users
  Constituency (NCUC) 82, 90–91
"non-paper" 103, 111
non-state actors 4, 48
NordNet (Sweden) 47
norms 17, 25, 147
North America 130
Norway 116, 127
not-for-profit standard-setting
  bodies, ensure that proprietary
  software compatible 40
NSF 33, 51–52
NSI 50–52, 155n4
Numbers Resource organization
  116
Nzépa, Oliver Nana 116

official publications, compete with
  electronically available
  information xiii
old system ineffective, borderless
  nature of Internet 24
open standards 137
Operative Point of Contact (OPOC)
  93
Optional Protocol, adopted by 123
  countries (October 2007) 67
Optional Protocol to the Convention
  on the Rights of the Child on the
  Sale of Children, Child
  Prostitution and Child
  Pornography 67
Organization of African Unity
  (OAU) internet Task Force 81
organizational involvement by issue
  area 18, **20–22**

packet switching, Internet based on 7
packet switching protocol 38
packets containing content, coded in
  sender's computer by e-mail or
  web-authoring programs 10
Pakistan 120
Panos Institute (West
  Africa – CIPACO Project) 133
Paris Convention for the Protection
  of Industrial Property (patents)
  29
Parisi, Dan, archetypical
  cybersquatter 61

Peake, Adam 130
peer-to-peer sharing (P2P), issues of
  fair use 62
Pegasus (Australia) 47
phishing, crime involving e-mail to
  fool people into providing bank
  details 67–68
phone system numbering plan, break
  down with rise of wireless cellular
  systems 9
pipes, fiber-optic cable network
  owned by private companies 10
Pisanty, Alejandro 79, 118
Plain Old Telephone Service *see*
  POTS
Plan of Action, ideas from Civil
  Society Coalition 106, 158n13;
  UN to set up working group on
  Internet governance 18, 152n8
plenary discussions in MAG, broad
  issue clusters 130
Pokey and the Madonna.com
  problem 60–61
Policy Advisory Board, MoU and
  52, 55
Policy Oversight Committee (POC)
  52, 55
Population Communication-
  International 100
Portugal 140
postal rates, mechanisms 16
Postel, Professor Jon (University of
  Southern California) 12, 50, 71–73,
  89
POTS, communication over the
  Internet similar to 6
principles 17, 25, 147
privacy 137
Private, bottom-up coordination 56
private computer corporations,
  proprietary applications for which
  consumers pay 40
private corporations, joined not-for-
  profit standard-setting bodies 40, 42
private sector 2, 18; "green"
  technology and carbon emissions
  150
Protocol Supporting Organization
  77–78, 83
Public Policy 17–18

Al-Qaida, attack on United States 11 September 2001 by use of Internet 67
quadrennial Plenipotentiary Conference in Minneapolis (Minnesota), ITU and 97
Qualcomm, monopoly in mobile phone technology 40, 42
Quaynor, Nii 79, 81
questionnaire, WGIG members and 120, 159n23

Rawalpindi Amateur Theatrical Society (RATS) 30–31
receiver 12–13, 15–16
Recording industry Association of America (RIAA) 63
regime theory, defines what has to be agreed 17, 147
regimes to govern the Internet, similar to older information and communications technologies xv
Registered Name Holders 92–93
registering domain names for a fee, major cash cow for NSI by (1997) 51
Registrars Constituency 82
Registry Constituency 82
regulation, order in telecommunications and in intellectual property 24
regulatory decision, solved problem of who would be registers 14
RELease (online journal) 74
Representation 56–57
Resource Allocation and Assignment 17–18
Right to Communicate 107
Rights, Responsibilities and Governance theme 105, 158n11
Rio de Janeiro, 2007 Internet Governance Forum 126, 138; critical Internet resources discussed 145; plenary sessions and session on critical Internet resources 140; second meeting of IGF (November 2007) 5; structure of Forum 138–39
Rio environmental conference (1992) 109

RIPE NCC (Europe), Robert Blokzijil 78
Roberts, Michael M. 74–75, 82
Root Server System Advisory Committee (RSSAC) 82–83
"rough consensus", alternative method of domain registry 52; IETF process 35–36, 154n3
routers, key to delivering packets to destination 7–10, 152n2
Royal Institute of International Affairs 121
rules 17
Russian Federation 62, 136
Rutkowski, Tony (first executive director of the Internet Society) 2, 72, 151n3

Saudi Arabia 120, 136
Schechter, Michael 97, 158n1
Science Applications International Corporation (SAIC) 50
Second prescriptive sentence 119
secretary-general, should examine IGF 124
Security and Stability Advisory Committee (SSAC) 82
sender/receiver, unlocatable in conventional spatial sense 10
senders 6–7, 12–14
server 38
"Setting the Scene" 132
Sharman Systems using software KaZaA, sued by RIAA for P2P sharing of music 63
Siemens 127
Singh, Parinder Jeet 134
Sklarov, Dmitry (Russian programmer), copyright violation charge 64, 156n7
Skype (Global P2P Telephony Company) 43
Slaughter, Anne Marie 148, 160n3
"social networking" sites like MySpace and YouTube, copyright issues 64
Solomon, Richard Jay 43
Sony Corp. of America vs. Universal City Studios Inc., "Betamax Case" 29, 61

South Africa 140
space satellites for communication, ITU allocated geo-stationary orbit slots 26
spam 67, 129, 137
spammers, access e-mail addresses using "bots" 67
spectrum allocation and orbit slots, involved dividing up scarce goods 26
stability 56
standards, process of agreeing on organized since 1996 34, 154n2
states, allowed to tap telephone calls 27
Sterling, Bruce, law enforcement in United States 23, 152n11
Stevens, Ted (US senator from Alaska), telecommunications bill 1–2, 4, 151n1
Stewart, Justice Potter, difficulty in defining pornography 66
stocktaking, preceded by closed meeting of MAG 135
streaming video, required more bandwidth 142
Supporting Organizations, dominated by representatives of private corporations 74, 77, 83, 90
Swiss Education and Research Network (SWITCH) 116
Swiss Federal Institute of Technology, "Internet Governance and Security" 138
Switzerland 101, 103, 127
Syracuse University and Georgia Tech (US) 4, 127
Syracuse University School of Information Studies 138
Syria 120

Taiwan, participates in GAC meetings as does China 89
Taiwan Province of China (.tw) 89
TCP/IP, software that allowed data to pass from one computer to another over communication lines 32
TCP/IP network, designers reserved 32 bits for packet address 7

Technical Architecture Group (TAG) 40
Technical Liaison Group (TLG) 82
Technical Management Board 71
Technical Standardization 17–18
technical standards: the engineers 33–37
Technical University of Berlin 4
technology, packets reassembled in right order and not corrupted by data error 10
Teldesic and Motorola, communications satellites in orbit 15
Telecom companies, privatized 98
Telecommunications, companies 40, 43; deregulation changed nature of stakeholders in ITU 98; monopolies as an issue of competition 16; technology intersecting with recognized global commons 15
telegraph lines, did not run over national boundaries 24
telephone system addressing system, Sally asking operator to connect her to Harry 9
Telephone and Telegraph Consultative Committee (CCITT) 26
telephony 10, 26
terrorism, problem of definition 67
"the way forward" 132, 134
Third World Institute (ITeM) 133
Third World Network 137
three PrepComs and WGIG consultations, well attended 122–23
Title II, all persons have right to correspond by international telegraphs 25
Trade-Related Aspects of Intellectual property Rights *see* TRIPS
trademarked names, problems of 51
trademarks, distinguish products of one company from another 28
traditional telephone conversation, what you need 6
Transmission Control Protocol/Internet Protocol *see* TCP/IP

TRIPS 27, 30, 61
Truscott, Tom 44
Tunis Agenda for Information
    Society 124–25, 127, 159n29
Tunis summit 112; avoided critical
    Internet resources 140; Internet
    governance and 126; (November
    2005) 3, 5, 101; preparatory
    Committee meeting (13–15
    November) 124; PrepCom for
    summit in Tunisia (24–26 June
    2004) 116; result of summit 125;
    second phase of WSIS in (2005)
    112; WGIG report basis of
    negotiation for 122
Tunisia 101, 103
Twomey, Paul (CEO of ICANN) 83,
    87–88, 120, 132

UN, states tend to negotiate through
    groups 117
UN Division for Economic and
    Social Council Support and
    Coordination 99
UN ICT Task Force, ECOSOC
    discussion and 114
UN Millennium Summit
    (September), adopted
    Millennium Development Goals
    100
UN women's conferences 108–9
UNCED 47
UNESCO 27, 139
UNICT, "A Grand Collaboration"
    4, 151n4; forum on Internet
    governance (April 2004) 5
UNICT Task Force (2004) 17, 152n7
Uniform Dispute Resolution Process
    (UDRP) 60–61, 74
United Kingdom 127
United Nations, engaged with
    information and communications
    technology 99; two-day
    consultation (February 2006) in
    Geneva 127
United Nations Commission on
    Science and Technology for
    Development 5
United Nations Conference on
    Human Rights in Vienna 47

United Nations Conference on
    Trade and Development 99
United Nations Economic and
    Social Council 47
United Nations Educational
    Scientific and Cultural
    Organization *see* UNESCO
United Nations Framework
    Convention on Climate Change
    149–50
United Nations human rights
    program 27
United Nations Information and
    Communications Technology
    Task Force *see* UNICT
United States 54, 132; after invading
    Iraq became suspect in
    multilateral circles 4;
    communication run by private
    corporations 25; decided to accept
    Postel group to create ICANN 73;
    defended WTO and WIPO in
    Paris consultations 107; delegation
    to ITU did not sign MoU 53;
    deregulation of telecommunications
    42; disputes on intellectual
    property resolved nationally 29;
    kept distance from WGIG and
    continued to protect ICANN 123;
    members of W3C from private
    corporations 39; new approach to
    governance 49; NSF and 33; party
    to Convention on Cybercrime 68;
    presidential election 2008 may
    change parameters of issues 144;
    responsibility for assigning names
    50; sued Microsoft 40; used.us to
    register secondary schools 88; .xxx
    domain name and 95
United States, Canada, United
    Kingdom, Ghana and Japan,
    board of CPSR 47
United States Department of
    Defense 32
United States Supreme Court,
    copyright infringement and 61–62,
    64; *MGM Studios v. Grokster*, 125
    S. Ct. 2764 (2005) 63;
    pornographic film (Jacobellis vs.
    Ohio, 378 US. 184 (1964)) 66

Universal Declaration on Human
Rights (1948), civil and political
rights (Article 19) 27, 66
Universal Postal Union (UPU) xv, 25
Uruguay 133
US Defense Department's Arpanet,
unlimited number of packets over
same circuit with different
addresses 7
US Department of Defense,
guaranteed integrity of Internet
scheme 9
US Federal Court, Fantasy vs.
Fogerty, 510 US. 517 (1994) 65
Usenet, network run by volunteers
with common interests 44, 47
Utsumi, Yoshio 99–100, 158n8

Verizon Foundation 127
"visionaries panel" and series of
thematic roundtables 104
Voice Over Internet protocols (voip)
43

W3C 37–38, 120, 127, 130; country
of member residency by
organization **39**; formal decision-
making structure 40; major
agreements on web protocols
40–41, 154n10; membership
(September 2007) **39**; rough
consensus 147; supported by
DARPA and the European
Commission 38, 154n8
Web networks (Canada) 47
Western Europe 130
WGIG 112–13, 116–22, 128;
alternative definitions, descriptive
and prescriptive 119, 159n21;
Chatham House Rule 121; entire
discussions transcribed 129;
follow-up to WSIS and 120; issue
of size 117; multi-stakeholder
body 112; oversight mechanisms
and forum structure 122;
patronage of UN secretary-
general 114; policy issues for
Internet governance 18, 113,
152n10; proposed IGF would
follow model of 125; report as

basis of final negotiation for Tunis
summit 122; secretariat prepared
section-by section compilation of
comments 122, 159n27; series of
12 papers in session from 18–20
April 2005 119; Tunis (November
2005) 3; voluntary funding 116, 127
White Paper 56–58, 96–97, 155n8;
consensus-based approach to new
institutions 73; on governance and
ICANN 70, 80, 88, 157n2; major
section on globalization 57;
private initiatives to create new
institution 72
WHOIS database 76, 92–93, 158n23
Wikipedia, describes Usenet 44,
154n16
WIPO 27, 128; (1967) 29; case of
Madonna Ciccone against Dan
Parisi 60–61; difficulty with
intellectual property 120; initial
proposals by resisted 76; to
manage dispute resolution
mechanism 52; trademark
disputes and 57; UDRP and
ICANN 76
wireless transmission, international
"space" and 15, 43
Woman Action 2000 100
women, MAG and 130
Working Group on Internet
Governance *see* WGIG
workshop organizers, report to the
plenary 131
World Bank 99
World Bank/UNDP/Canada Global
Knowledge '97 Conference 16
World Conference on Human Rights
(Austria) 101
World Economic Forum 146, 160n1
World Information Transfer 100
World Intellectual Property
Organization *see* WIPO
World Meteorological Organization
150
World Summit on the Information
Society *see* WSIS
World Trade Organization *see* WTO
World Wide Web Consortium *see*
W3C

Worldbank Infodev TAP 81
WSIS 3–4, 96, 116, 119, 126, 128,
    136; (2003) governance and 97;
    conference and agenda of UN
    System Chief Executive Board 98,
    158n4; Declaration finally agreed
    by 111–12; definition of the
    Internet 6; enabling regulatory
    and policy framework suggested
    103, 158n9; envisaged long
    preparatory process 102; (Geneva
    2003) 18, 61; global coordination
    of Internet's underlying resources
    113; Internet governance emerged
    from (November 2003) 4;
    mentioned intellectual property
    only twice 61; multi-stakeholder
    forum meeting Athens (November
    2006) 3; second phase in Tunis
    (2005) 112; Tunisia (November
    2005) 5; United Nations rules and
    108
WSIS Declaration of Principles,
    "agreed text" 122
WSIS I: Internet governance
    emerges 102–4
WSIS II, preparations for 113
WTO 99, 120, 128, 154n11; adopted
    agreements on TRIPS 61;
    agreement on TRIPS negotiated
    in Uruguay Round (1986–94) 27,
    30

YouTube 64–65, 133

Zittrain, Jonathan 78